DATE DUE

~~MY 21 97~~		
MY 26 '98		
~~OC 20 '98~~		
~~NO 20 '98~~		
AG 7 '0		

DEMCO 38-296

RED FLAG OVER HONG KONG

Red Flag over Hong Kong

Bruce Bueno de Mesquita
David Newman
Alvin Rabushka

CHATHAM HOUSE PUBLISHERS, INC.
CHATHAM, NEW JERSEY

RED FLAG OVER HONG KONG

Chatham House Publishers, Inc.
Box One, Chatham, New Jersey, 07928

Publisher: Edward Artinian
Production supervisor: David Morris
Jacket and cover design: Lawrence Ratzkin
Composition: Bang, Motley, Olufsen
Printing and binding: R.R. Donnelley & Sons, Co.

LIBRARY OF CONGRESS CATALOGING-IN-PUBLICATION DATA

Bueno de Mesquita, Bruce, 1946–
    Red flag over Hong Kong / Bruce Bueno de Mesquita, David
Newman, Alvin Rabushka.
        p.   cm.
    Includes bibliographical references (p.   ) and index.
    ISBN 1-56643-041-0 (cloth). — ISBN 1-56643-040-2 (pbk.)
    1. Hong Kong—Politics and government—Forecasting. 2. China—
Politics and government—1976– —Forecasting. I. Newman, David,
1956– . II. Rabushka, Alvin. III. Title.
DS796.H757B85   1996
303.495125—dc20   95-50248
                                                            CIP

MANUFACTURED IN THE UNITED STATES OF AMERICA
10   9   8   7   6   5   4   3   2   1

Contents

PART TWO
FORECASTING THE FUTURE

APPENDIXES

Figures

Preface

On 1 July 1997 two red flags will fly over Hong Kong. One is the red flag with five yellow stars of the People's Republic of China. The other is the red flag with a single bauhinia flower of the Hong Kong Special Administrative Region, the new political entity that will supplant the British Crown Colony of Hong Kong. As those two flags are hoisted, and as the Union Jack is lowered for the last time at Government House, a profound political transition will occur. The United Kingdom, which has governed Hong Kong since 1841, will transfer sovereignty and administrative responsibility over Hong Kong to the government of mainland China. The Chinese Communist Party will replace Her Majesty's government as the ultimate font of power and authority.

Six million Hong Kong residents wait with growing apprehension. Although China has promised to preserve Hong Kong's capitalistic system for fifty years and to allow Hong Kong's people a high degree of autonomy, the Chinese Communist Party and the Central People's Government in Beijing are better known for their disregard of human rights; the Tiananmen Square incident of 4 June 1989, in which tanks and soldiers opened fire on unarmed civilians; systemic corruption in economic life; and intolerance of individual freedom.

"To Go or Stay" is the title of chapter 1 because that is the choice that faces upward of a million middle-class, English-educated Hong Kong residents. Will they stay because they believe China's promises? Or will they go because they do not trust China?

Red Flag over Hong Kong is a handbook about the future of Hong Kong. It seeks to inform the colony's articulate, prosperous middle class, the international business community that has a stake in Hong Kong and East Asia, and the overseas Chinese who have dispersed to every part of the globe from Hong Kong. Since events in China will ultimately determine Hong Kong's future, it is also a guide to the future of China. *Red Flag over Hong Kong* will be one of many guides published in the remaining months before 1 July 1997. But *Red Flag* is unique because our forecasts on future developments in China and Hong Kong rest on an explicit model of decision making (see appendix B), not on access to insiders or the divination of tea leaves. This model has established a remarkable record of real-time predictive accuracy over a wide range of political issues in many parts of the world. The model depends on the collection of data from "experts" who study given countries and important issues. The experts who provided the data for our book represent the business, academic, media, and political sectors of Hong Kong.

We sent the manuscript to the publisher in November 1995. There is a temptation to hold the manuscript one more day, every day, to include the latest event, pronouncement, transgression, or statistic. Each new development seems more important than the last, especially in Hong Kong's dynamic circumstances. No doubt many interesting events will have taken place in 1996 that are not included in *Red Flag*. But our purpose was to provide readers in Hong Kong, and those around the world concerned about its people and economy, with as early a set of forecasts as possible.

We have not cluttered the text with scores of footnotes. Any important references are cited directly in the text and can easily be found in any major university library. Most of the specific events we mention were initially reported in various issues of the *Far Eastern Economic Review* and the *South China Morning Post*, the two most important sources of information about Hong Kong in English, and *The Economist*. The Government Information Services of the Hong Kong government publishes an annual report, which is a comprehensive overview of the territory's political, social, and economic development of the past year. We made extensive use of *Hong Kong 1995: A Review of 1994*. Statistics of China's economic development were taken from the annual report of China's State Statistical Bureau. Both the *Singapore Business Times* and the *Hongkong Tiger Standard* have home pages on the Internet, which provide daily summaries of the main political and economic news in Hong Kong and China. Other sources include official documents, especially the texts of the Joint Declaration, which is reproduced as appendix A, and the Basic Law.

We have lots of organizations and people to thank. Bruce Bueno de Mesquita and Alvin Rabushka are comfortably ensconced at the Hoover Institution, where they enjoy outstanding facilities and research support, which made work on this book possible. David Newman thanks the Staff Development and Scholarly Activities Committee of Lingnan College for financial support. We thank Decision Insights Incorporated of Reston, Virginia, for permission to use its proprietary software of the model on which the forecasts were derived. We thank David Weimer and

Brian Bridges for their comments on various portions of the manuscript. We thank our experts who supplied the data inputs for the model. Without their expertise, the abstract logic in the model could not have generated concrete forecasts. We thank Chatham House and its publisher, Edward Artinian, who shared our enthusiasm for this project. We, not they, of course, are responsible for the facts, interpretations, and conclusions in our book.

*Perchance to dream of
the Duke of Chou*

Part One

Background to Hong Kong

❋ 1 ❋

To Go or Stay?

1 July 1997. At 12:00:01 A.M., the new Hong Kong will begin. The old Hong Kong, the last British Crown Colony in Asia, will be no more. A new China will emerge, another step taken in the inexorable process of national reunification. China awaits only the return of the Portuguese territory of Macao, scheduled for 1999, and the resolution of the issue of Taiwan to complete its extension of sovereignty to all the territory it claims. In its view, China's takeover of Hong Kong finally puts right the wrongs of the Opium Wars by removing the last major stain of foreign rule on Chinese soil.

CNN will be there, along with CBS, NBC, ABC, ITN, the BBC, and camera crews from around the world. Foreign ministers will fly in to witness the moment. Chinese and British dignitaries will make speeches at numerous ceremonies, lunches, and dinners. Champagne and brandy will flow freely as the People's Liberation Army parades along Queen's Road, perhaps newly renamed Reunification Boulevard. Millions of Hong Kong residents will line the streets waving two red flags—one with five yellow stars and the other, Hong Kong's new red flag with a single bauhinia (a beautiful flower similar to an orchid). In pomp and circumstance, the day will surpass the festivities that established the People's Republic of China in Beijing on 1 October 1949.

Every hotel room is sold out for 30 June 1997. Every penthouse restaurant or harbor-view suite is reserved for what will be the most spectacular fireworks display in Asian history. Money will be no object as Hong Kong's millionaires strive to outdo one another in hosting the grandest party and showing support for the new Hong Kong. The celebrations of 1 July 1997 may well be the most flamboyant peaceful political orgy in history.

2 July 1997. Another story will begin—and with a massive political hangover. After the sanitation department has swept up the party debris strewn all over town, 6 million Hong Kong residents will arise

to a new polity. The last of the high-level English-speaking, expatriate civil servants will be airborne. In their place will be a new set of administrators, taking their cues not from London or even from Hong Kong's elected legislators, all of whom China has promised to replace, but from high Communist Party officials in Beijing.

Good riddance to the *gwailos,* or foreign devils, as the Cantonese call them. Every Chinese will no doubt feel patriotic tugs of race, language, culture, and motherland. But life goes on, discovering a new normalcy. People will get up in the morning, shower, shave, dress, go to work, go shopping, prepare dinner, watch television, read the newspaper, and go to bed. How much of the old normalcy will remain and how much will change are the questions on the minds of 6 million people.

What is normal in Hong Kong? Normal is stability and prosperity, economic opportunity, free speech, a free press, academic freedom, freedom of travel, the rule of law, and an efficient and honest civil service. If things go well, all these will continue.

What if things go badly? What recourse will be there for the people of Hong Kong? Will they be able to petition their government for a redress of grievances? Will they be permitted to emigrate? Will they be allowed to sue corrupt officials in the courts? Will they be able to compete fairly against mainland business firms that operate in Hong Kong? Will they be able to educate their children in English? Will they be able to invest their savings outside Hong Kong?

The world is a different place today than it was in 1950. Back then, few people traveled abroad or had television; only a few knew where Hong Kong was or had ever been there. Today is the world of the Internet and instant communication. Every literate person knows where Hong Kong is, and millions have gone there for business or pleasure. Its skyline and harbor are familiar landmarks. What happens in Hong Kong will be of interest to the rest of the world. In particular, investors will watch with great care what happens to the people of Hong Kong because their fate is an early warning of China's future path.

1 July 1997 marks a political watershed, the transfer of 6 million people from Britain's rule to China's. The world's oldest parliamentary democracy will abandon 6 million *free* people to a regime born of revolution, which respects the use of force, not the rule of law. Everyone who knows Hong Kong has an opinion on its future—some are optimistic, more pessimistic. But the takeover of a people by a different government has historical precedent.

Remember, China itself underwent a takeover by a different government in 1949. Consider a conversation among businessmen in Shanghai in 1949 as the Communist Party seized power. What might they have said or thought? "The defeated Nationalists were corrupt and deserved their fate. The Communists are men of their word. They say they will rely upon us Shanghainese with our business acumen to help rebuild China. They have promised that we will be allowed to keep our businesses and property. We are patriotic Chinese, after all, and love our motherland."

It is not necessary to imagine conversations that have been and are taking place among Hong Kong's 6 million people during the 1990s. We have heard them with our own ears. "It is right to end colonial rule." "China has promised us that we can run our own affairs under their policy of *one country, two systems,* which is enshrined in the Basic Law, Hong Kong's new constitution." "China honors its treaties." "China says that we can maintain our capitalist way of life for fifty years, until 2047." "China says that we can maintain our social, economic, and political systems and that the socialist policies of the mainland will not be applied to Hong Kong." "The Chinese need our capital, know-how, entrepreneurial talents, worldwide trading links, and goodwill to continue their current reform program." "They would never kill the goose that lays the golden eggs; they need Hong Kong for their own development." "We know the leaders in Beijing on a first-name basis. We can place a phone call to resolve any problems that affect our business affairs in China. We have good connections." "We can cope with a small increase in corruption and bribery." "Chinese culture doesn't place much importance on so-called Western civil liberties, so Hong Kong people are not concerned about losing these so-called freedoms. Besides, the British colonial rulers never allowed us Chinese to fully realize our capabilities."

In quiet whispers, we also hear Hong Kong people say, "We have foreign passports, green cards, or enough money to get out if things go bad." "I'm old, so I don't mind staying, but my children are safely in the United States." "My personal wealth is in the Cayman Islands. I keep in Hong Kong banks only what I need to pay monthly bills." "My goodness, Hong Kong's richest billionaire, Li Ka-Shing, put his $1.7 billion in shares in a trust somewhere in the West Indies. Everyone knows it's not for tax reasons."

The future of Hong Kong will become an industry in itself—in what's left of Hong Kong's colonial future. Everyone in the business of political or economic forecasting will issue a report on the future of Hong Kong. During the last days of British rule, the shops will overflow with books, magazines, journals, and newspapers on Hong

Kong's future. Television and radio talk shows will interview pundits who dissect public opinion polls. Predictions will range from euphoric to "the death of Hong Kong." How is one to choose among the scenarios?

In 1985 we published a book entitled *Forecasting Political Events: The Future of Hong Kong.* The research and analysis for that book were completed in March 1984, six months before the Chinese and the British announced the terms of their agreement for the future of Hong Kong. The book contained forecasts covering such topics as sovereignty, a continued British administrative presence in Hong Kong, Hong Kong's free-market economy, protection of civil liberties, the courts, the Hong Kong currency, land leases, the tax system, and labor regulations. We also explained in detail the technique we used to make our forecasts. That technique is based on a model that captures the *logic* of collective decision making. It does not depend on personal contacts or access to "insider" information. We have not met, or spoken with, the leaders of China or Hong Kong.

The forecasts we made in 1984 look very good in 1996. But the data we collected from "experts" in 1984 are outdated. We decided it would be useful to focus our attention once again on Hong Kong using new "expert" information and an improved version of our forecasting technique (see appendix B).

The Last Fifteen Years

In the early 1980s, when the future of Hong Kong came up for serious discussion between Britain and China, the fifteen years that remained until 1997 seemed an eternity. There was plenty of money yet to be made in Hong Kong. Britain was firmly in charge, and Margaret Thatcher was at her peak following Britain's victory in the Falkland Islands. China, in contrast, was at a low point. Deng Xiaoping had just launched his economic reforms. The Hong Kong business community was powerful in its own right. Other groups—expatriate civil servants, mid-level civil servants, intellectuals—were also important in the discussion.

By the mid-1990s, the tables have turned. Britain is in charge of Hong Kong in name only. Mrs. Thatcher is gone, and her successor, John Major, has presided over a steady fall in the fortunes of the Tories. Chris Patten, the governor of Hong Kong, has been cursed and browbeaten by Chinese leaders high and low—unimaginable a decade ago. China has broken many promises it made to the people of Hong Kong. The local business community is bigger and richer than ever, playing a major role in China's development. China, in contrast, is much stronger and more powerful than it was in 1982, having achieved spectacular growth in recent years. Mainland firms and millionaires reflect a proud, powerful China.

What do these changes mean for Hong Kong? Simply this: events in China, not in Britain, Hong Kong, or anywhere else, will dictate the future of Hong Kong. John Major, the Tories, and the British government have no direct influence. Power resides within China and is shared among the new generation of leaders of the Chinese Communist Party, old party hard-liners, the political military, and the new breed of military business firms. In addition, rival interests have sprung to life in the high-growth coastal provinces of Guangdong, Fujian, and Shanghai.

To be sure, Hong Kong will still feel the effects of global recession, changes in interest rates, and new technology. But the fundamental institutions of its government, society, and economy will be shaped by Chinese interests. The future of Hong Kong, one step removed, is the future of China.

Mass Emigration

Since the early 1980s, every year tens of thousands of Hong Kong residents have emigrated to the United States, Canada, Australia, and Britain. In all, more than half a million Hong Kong residents have acquired foreign nationality or residence. Some are back in Hong Kong to make money, but their wives and children remain abroad. Hong Kong has always been a staging ground for emigration, but the mass exodus did not begin until 1997 started to get close.

How many people can leave Hong Kong?

Almost everyone with money or skills. It is estimated that as many as 1 million people have foreign passports, foreign resident permits, options to emigrate, or the educational or financial resources to find some hospitable foreign shore. The other 5 million who hold Hong Kong identity or travel documents, which become meaningless after 1997, could choose to become the next wave of boat people, taking their chances in Taiwan, the Philippines, or even Southeast Asia.

How many will leave? That depends. Most of the people who make their home in Hong Kong love it. They delight in the crowds, the nightlife, the restaurants, the feverish pace of life—the sheer excitement of it all—and, of course, in making money. There is no other Hong Kong anywhere else in the world. If Hong Kong retains its current normalcy, most will stay, and others who have left may return.

The crucial question is whether Hong Kong will stay normal. Virtually every Chinese resident of Hong Kong has parents or grandparents who fled mainland China for the safety of Hong Kong. Some fled to Hong Kong in the 1920s to escape warlords. Some fled in the 1930s to escape the Japanese. Some fled in the 1940s to escape the civil war. Some fled in the 1950s to escape the communists.

Since 1980, when Deng opened up the Chinese economy, more than a million Hong Kong residents have visited China to see firsthand how China's people work and live. The majority of Hong Kong's residents are well informed about conditions in China, though many keep their opinions to themselves. Probably all residents of Hong Kong more than ten years old watched the horror show that took place in Tiananmen Square in June 1989; they saw China's leaders send tanks and troops against students to suppress a growing movement for democracy.

The casual visitor might come away from Hong Kong convinced that its largely Cantonese population cares only about making money. As long as Hong Kong remains stable and prosperous, the Cantonese will keep quiet and let the communists have their way. But this impression is wrong. The Cantonese speakers, the great majority of Hong Kong's Chinese population, love freedom as much as any Western people. The potential loss of freedom, not a slowdown in the Hong Kong economy, poses the greatest risk to the territory's future.

A Preview —
China after Deng

We present a preview of our main findings in this introduction. Since events in China will both constrain and drive events in Hong Kong, let us begin with the political and economic future of China.

Deng Xiaoping wanted to witness, personally, the return of Hong Kong to China. Whether or not he lives to see 1 July 1997, his rule is effectively over. Who will eventually succeed Deng, and will they maintain his policies within China and his promises to Hong Kong? Will the succession produce an autocrat, a team of party leaders, a return to power of the Old Guard, a new military-business alliance, or some other arrangement? How long will it take for the dust to settle?

Our prediction is as follows: The succession will be clouded by severe infighting among the politicized leaders in the military, the new business entrepreneurs within the military, and the main factions within the Communist Party—those headed by Jiang Zemin, Li Peng, the "Old Guard," and the ideological hard-liners. Added to this combustible mix will be a new force—the newly emergent, economically robust coastal provinces. After several rounds of brutal exchanges interrupted by pauses (like a boxing match), the party, in a deal with the regional leadership, will hold on to some power and perhaps nobody will win. During the uncertain process of succession, the business climate will be damaged. The military, the People's Liberation Army (PLA), will redirect its desire to participate in and influence civilian affairs; it will become a pragmatic, rather than ideological, military organization. The party has tried to curtail the boom in military entrepreneurship, but parts of the PLA will cooperate with provincial leaders in their struggle with the party. The result will be that authority at the center will be weakened. The coastal provinces will grow in power but will not fully supplant the party at least for several years.

What does it mean for the military to put business ahead of ideology? Doing so helps professionalize the military so that the PLA returns to soldiering. An important part of that soldiering is to protect the PLA's "right" to participate in business. Lining his pockets is more important to the "professional" soldier than is upholding communist orthodoxy. By giving up its ideological ties, the PLA fosters conflict between the party and regional interests, especially over command of economic matters. The party, as mentioned, is a mix of new and old, pragmatic and ideological, reformers and old-line socialists. It matters which individual, faction, or mix of members emerges as the effective leadership.

During his waning years, Deng Xiaoping has made economic reform his primary focus. Unfortunately, the party is not united behind his vision. The proponents of reform are Deng's still faithful followers in the party and the military entrepreneurs, the professional military, which sees a strong economy as the backbone of a strong military. Others are not supportive. Neither Jiang Zemin, Li Peng, nor the hard-liners favor the fast pace of reform. They do not wish to roll back the reforms, but they want to consolidate the progress to date before launching new measures. The upshot, we predict, is that there will be a moratorium on economic reform until the next century. Those who tied their bets on Hong Kong to economic reform in China will have to hold their breath for some time. China's economy will slow, and Hong Kong's along with it. This slowdown will result both from changes in official policy and from the substantial uncertainty fostered by the period of political turmoil.

In fact, the new China will be as different from the old China as the new Hong Kong will be from the old. By far the most important change, we predict, will be the loss of considerable power and influence by the central government in Beijing, while the dynamic regions—Shanghai, Fujian, Guangdong—will gain power. China after Deng will look more like the thirteen American colonies under the Articles of Confederation than the United States of America looks today under the Constitution. Or it might resemble the Swiss Confederation or even the feudal monarchies of Europe's Middle Ages. Taxation and welfare, to name two issues, will become increasingly local, not national, matters.

As a result of this development, the people of Hong Kong will have to look over both shoulders at the same time; over one to Beijing, over the other to Shanghai, Xiamen, and Canton. The people of Hong Kong will be caught in the struggle between Beijing and the affluent regions each going its own way. Autonomy from Beijing could mean incorporation into Guangdong. Protection from Canton might require an alliance with Beijing. These are not easy shoals to navigate.

Finally, the most important issue that defines the relationship of Hong Kong to China—autonomy. Will Hong Kong people govern Hong Kong? Or will China call the shots?

Coming Attraction— Hong Kong after Deng

The result, like a Chinese dish, is sweet and sour. In the early rounds of political maneuvering in China, Hong Kong enjoys substantial autonomy, but that autonomy is short-lived, precipitously collapses, and finally, disappears. On 1 July 1997 Hong Kong will change from a British Crown Colony to a special administrative region (SAR) of China. The new Hong Kong SAR will be governed by a Basic Law enacted by the National People's Congress in Beijing on 4 April 1990. The Basic Law promises Hong Kong a high degree of autonomy for at least fifty years, but this promise is empty.

The devil of Hong Kong's future is in the details. Autonomy is a vague concept and can mean different things to different people. The freedom to make money may be enough autonomy for businessmen. For professors and students in Hong Kong's universities, autonomy may mean the right to criticize China without troops and tanks being sent to campuses. For the media, autonomy may mean no censorship. For the Hong Kong monetary authority, autonomy may mean a separate Hong Kong dollar, backed by U.S. dollars, not China's renminbi currency. For local politicians, autonomy may mean free and fair elections, while for justices and lawyers, autonomy may mean an independent, impartial judiciary. For local businessmen, autonomy may mean an equal playing field, without favoritism for mainland firms. For the taxpayer, autonomy may mean an efficient, honest civil service, especially a reliable, honest police force. For workers, autonomy may mean the right to organize labor unions.

The preview of coming attractions in Hong Kong after 1 July 1997 is not auspicious. Here we summarize our forecasts. Chapters 5 and 6 of this book present the full analysis on which the forecasts rest, with supporting material in appendix B.

THE ECONOMY

We begin with the economy. The most telling characteristic of Hong Kong is its robust economy. Per capita income in Hong Kong is higher than in Britain—indeed, higher than in most Western countries. This is due to the workings of a free-market economy, a recipe that includes low taxes, limited government, sound money, and free trade. Stability and prosperity have always been the most highly valued features of the territory, so much so that the local population, it is supposed, will sacrifice a great many things, including political and civil rights, for economic prosperity. The first, and perhaps most salient question, is what will be the future direction of the economy.

Will Hong Kong maintain its free-market policies? The answer is that the new government, controlled by Chinese interests, will impose increasingly severe restrictions on the economy. Within a decade, the free market will be significantly curtailed.

How will the Hong Kong economy look in 2007? The simple answer is more and more like Shenzhen and Canton. These two Chinese cities across the border in Guangdong will continue to develop as Hong Kong loses its vitality and begins to stagnate.

One reason for a slowdown in Hong Kong is that foreign firms will be encouraged to move inland; purely local Hong Kong firms will not enjoy a level playing field with mainland firms or firms with mainland connections. Equal treatment under the law will give way to accommodate the superior political status of mainland business interests.

POLITICAL FREEDOM

It would not be stretching the truth to say that from Hong Kong's founding in 1841 until the 1980s, Hong Kong's residents lived by bread alone. They were happy not to be involved in politics. To them, Hong Kong's great virtue was the absence of politics.

All that has changed. The last fifteen years of British rule in Hong Kong have been marked by intense politics. A formerly appointed legislature is now fully elected—a combination of twenty seats chosen from geographical constituencies, thirty seats from functional constituencies (professional groups), and ten seats indirectly chosen by directly elected members of District Boards (a form of local government). Local Hong Kong Chinese have formed political parties, and public opinion polls on political issues are commonplace. Criticism of the governor, his chief civil servants, and his policies is vocal inside the legislature and on the streets. The press openly criticizes government policies and high officials by name. The media give politics, especially current and future relations with China, far more coverage than they give economics. Talk on the street is about Hong Kong's political future, not its economy.

Apart from economic autonomy, how much political autonomy will Hong Kong have? Will Hong Kong get to exercise the political freedoms enumerated in the Basic Law, which gives the future Hong Kong the appearance of a Western-style democracy? Will political parties be free to organize, and will elections be free and fair? Will an elected legislature have the power to enact laws free from mainland interference or direction? Will the legislature do anything more than rubber-stamp the Chinese-appointed chief executive's proposals? And what about the chief executive himself? Will he be accountable to locally elected representatives and the people of Hong Kong, or will he take instructions from China?

Civil rights go hand in hand with political freedoms. Freedom of speech, of the press, of the universities, of travel, of assembly—these freedoms and others are essential in any free society. Without these civil rights, the exercise of democracy is a meaningless set of procedures that result in the rulers getting their way.

It is in the arenas of politics and human rights that mainland China has been most deficient. The Basic Law, and its predecessor, the Joint Declaration, spelled out a full set of political and civil liberties. On paper, Hong Kong people will enjoy a high degree of freedom, equaling that in the Western democracies. But China's own people have these same rights—on paper. Will Hong Kong's 6 million Chinese enjoy real liberty or just the paper rights that more than a billion of their compatriots have across the border?

Political parties will appear to have a modest degree of freedom. China will allow parties to organize and campaign, but the elections in which they participate will be controlled from the mainland. Hong Kong's parties will have only limited freedom to express critical views of China or even to challenge the bounds of political discourse that China places on issues that involve Hong Kong.

One reason that parties may appear slightly independent is that elections will not be free and fair. Mainland authorities will do whatever is required to get the outcome they want. A majority, or at least enough elected legislators, will support China to preclude legislative decisions that go against the mainland's wishes. China will not allow the Hong Kong legislature to be a political irritant. No more than a handful of anti-China candidates will be permitted to win office, and the few who do win will be tolerated only to create a veneer of legitimacy in world opinion.

The Basic Law stipulates that China will appoint a chief executive to replace the colonial governor. He "shall be selected by election or through consultations held locally and be appointed by the Central People's Government." Annex I in the Basic Law states that the election committee shall consist of 800 members. It specifies the committee's composition by occupation and political status. The selection of the 800 shall be prescribed by an electoral law enacted by the Hong Kong SAR. No dates are specified, nor is any deciding body in the Central People's Government.

We forecast that whoever is chosen, selected, or elected—take your pick—and appointed by the Central People's Government will have no independence. China will control him, and he will not be accountable to the people of Hong Kong. He will become a new breed of colonial governor, but more in keeping with the early days of Hong Kong when governors actually took instructions from London. China will place one or more political advisers in the governor's office and probably in his residence as well. The governor will need clearance before speaking or acting and will be about as independent as the erstwhile Chinese emperor of Manchukuo.

It is now clear that it does not matter how relations between the executive and legislative branches of the new Hong Kong are structured. On paper, the Basic Law assigns the chief executive thirteen powers and functions and gives ten to the legislature. But China's control of the chief executive and its virtual selection and control of the legislature renders moot a point of contention in most democracies: the distribution of power among different branches of government and the presence of checks and balances that limit one branch from gaining too much power.

The judiciary is a crucial branch of government in a democracy. It limits the power of both the legislature and the chief executive. In colonial Hong Kong, the judiciary has been independent of the executive and legislative councils, the bodies that set policies and enact laws. The courts, acting impartially, have protected individual rights and maintained a level playing field for business. In the new Hong Kong, the courts will try to maintain their independence and will be most successful in commercial adjudication. Nevertheless, they will not flout the will of China and will not arbitrate between the chief executive and the legislature. The court will not challenge the Communist Party leadership or government authorities in Beijing and Canton.

OTHER CONCERNS

The last set of forecasts on civil liberties are the bleakest. There will be no press freedom or academic freedom. The schools will become the educational tool of the state. The language of instruction and the curriculum will be set to serve mainland interests, not the interests of Hong Kong's 6 million people. Freedom to travel will gradually erode to mirror that granted to mainland residents. Labor unions will take their instructions from China, rather than serve the economic interests of their members.

The story is not yet complete. This book is also a survival kit for those who plan to remain or do business in Hong Kong. We explain how the international business and political community can, through concerted action, improve conditions in Hong Kong in all walks of life. Contrary to the received wisdom of most Sinologists, China would respond to international pressure on some issues to moderate its policies toward Hong Kong. Indeed, the survival of economic and political freedom in Hong Kong depends on the support of those outside Hong Kong who have a stake in the territory's future and the welfare of its residents. International efforts will be essential if Hong Kong is to continue to prosper. The international business and political communities will have to raise the costs for Chinese leaders if they renege on promises made to Hong Kong. If business and political concerns in the United States, Britain, Japan, and Taiwan look the other way, China will not be on good behavior. However sincere its intentions, the Chinese government will steadily abridge Hong Kong's future prospects if it is not continuously challenged and held accountable.

A couple of adages are useful guides to the meaning and direction of China's official statements. "Watch what people do; not what people say." "Talk is cheap; actions speak louder than words." Chinese officials are masterfully indifferent about saying one thing and doing something else. They are comfortable saying one thing today, something different tomorrow, still something else on the third day, only to repeat their position of the first day thereafter.

In December 1984 China and Britain signed the Joint Declaration, the document that sealed Hong Kong's fate. Hong Kong's mini-constitution, the Basic Law, was enacted in April 1990. Since then, local officials and elected politicians have expressed shock and disappointment each time China reneged on a promise or broke its word.

China's vacillations should come as no surprise. Despite opening the economy to market forces, China's leaders still espouse socialism and cling to its intellectual framework. Socialist thinking and action are not the same as capitalist thinking and action. Socialists live inside a Marxist framework of contradiction, of constantly shifting and conflicting realities, seeking to resolve the contradiction of the day. Above all, however, they do whatever it takes to retain power. Socialists, like many ideologues, find no shame in changing their words or policies every Monday and Thursday; unlike other ideologues, however, contradiction is inherent in their framework.

Western analysts may find all this shifting about inscrutable or illogical. But that is because they rely on an Aristotelian framework of logic and evidence to reason about China's behavior. They suppose that Chinese leaders think the same way they do. They hang on the latest word, the latest deed, the latest change in policy as harbingers of the future. Most analysts of China depend on inside information, divining from tea leaves as it were. They do not have a framework that allows them to escape the shifting currents of Chinese rhetoric and behavior. We do. Our framework allows for decision makers to renege on their promises and change their mind so long as those changes are consistent with their self-interest.

A few words about the structure of this book. This introductory chapter has previewed the questions we raise and our conclusions regarding Hong Kong's future. Chapter 2 explains how Hong Kong developed into one of the world's richest territories. Chapter 3 reviews modern China, first under the leadership of its "great helmsman" Mao Zedong and then under "pragmatist" Deng Xiaoping. Chapter 4 shifts back from China to Hong Kong. We ask a simple question: why would China risk the future of Hong Kong? The answer is that China's promises to Hong Kong consist of words that do not mean what words ordinarily mean, and China's actions belie the meaning of those words as they are understood in Western societies.

Chapters 5 and 6 present the hard analysis. Chapter 5 spells out China's future. Chapter 6 takes that future and superimposes it on Hong Kong. Chapter 7 presents the signposts of those futures in the next few years, what to look for when the red flag flies over Hong Kong—the decline of English, the shift of funds now held in Hong Kong by mainland firms and individuals to Singapore and other offshore locations, the rise of corruption, the suggestions for charitable contributions to "worthy" mainland organizations, and other internal developments. The book also includes two appendixes—the text of the Joint Declaration and a formal exposition of the forecasting model including descriptions of the data sets collected from experts about China and Hong Kong.

❊ 2 ❊

An Overview of Hong Kong

There is so much to see and do in 400 square miles. Parts of Hong Kong are pristine, rural, untouched islands with marvelous trails. Other parts overwhelm the senses, with more than a half million people crammed into a square mile of living and working space. The harbor is breathtaking by night and busy with commerce by day. Innovative architecture has displaced square blocks and Chinese shophouses. And everywhere there are people running from one place to another. Time is money, more so in Hong Kong than anywhere else, and time, like land, is scarce. It is running out.

There are so many tours to take in Hong Kong—the harbor tour, the New Territories tour, a day in China, Hong Kong at night, and the casinos in Macao. Each tour conveys bits and pieces of what Hong Kong is really all about.

Hong Kong is the *Guinness Book of Records*. It is the world's best example of the free-market economy, working as textbooks say it should. Neither time, money, nor effort is wasted. Risk takers abound in every nook and cranny. The Chinese people of Hong Kong have grown so rich that Mercedes Benz cars outnumber every other brand. The purpose of taking an economics tour, the subject of this chapter, is to highlight what is at stake and why Hong Kong's future matters to its 6 million people and the global business community.

Demography

Hong Kong is very small, just over 400 square miles. It consists of two large islands, many small ones, and a large continental land mass. The British occupied Hong Kong in stages, taking Hong Kong Island, today a center of finance and global business, in 1841. They grabbed Kowloon, now a shopping mecca across the harbor, in 1860, and in 1898 they extracted a ninety-nine-year lease for the New Territories, which consists of other islands and a continental land mass that extends to the Shenzhen River, Hong Kong's border with China.

There was never enough land in Hong Kong. It is mainly mountains of granite, thus largely unusable. The colonial government began reclaiming land almost immediately. In 1841 the waterfront of Hong Kong Island came up to the front door of the Hongkong and Shanghai Bank on Des Voeux Road Central. Today, it is blocks away. The colonial government reclaimed so much land in Hong Kong, and leveled so many mountains in the New Territories to create whole new cities, that the harbor itself is disappearing. A large part of the world's dredging fleet sits in Hong Kong waters extending shorelines to accommodate convention centers, hotels, office buildings, and a huge new airport.

There is not enough water in Hong Kong, necessitating that it be pumped in from China every day despite massive reservoir schemes all over the colony. The food and fish harvested in Hong Kong would feed only a handful of its people. There are no raw materials for industry. Every day, food, goods, machinery, and raw materials from all over the world are unloaded from trucks, trains, ships, and planes. When Captain Elliot took Hong Kong from China in 1841, he was roundly denounced in certain British quarters for having taken, in Lord Palmerston's words, "a barren island with hardly a house upon it."

Captain Elliot was no fool. He declared that Hong Kong would be free of tariffs. Free trade became a cornerstone of Hong Kong's economy. Trade grew so fast that the barren rock soon had tens of thousands of Chinese and European residents, trading to all corners of the globe. Hong Kong is still a duty-free port best known as a haven of tax-free shopping. Whatever you buy—suits, sweaters, jewelry, antiques, perfume —has no sales tax, export tax, import tax, or value-added tax.

Hong Kong opens a sophisticated shopping mall every week, or so it seems. Landmark, Lippo Center, Peregrine Center, United Tower, Pacific Place, Times Square, Causeway Bay, New World Center, Wing On Plaza, Tsim Sha Tsui Center, China Ferry Terminal, Kowloon City Plaza, Peak Shopping—the list goes on—outdo one another with the latest and most expensive in fashion, electronics, gourmet foods, and anything else money can buy. Any Hong Kong mall, even those in the New Territories or outlying islands, combines the best of New York, London, Paris, and Rome in one arcade.

Economic Policies

Economics is known as the dismal science. Reading about tax rates, budget outlays, and monetary policy is not as exciting as a murder mystery. For most visitors to Hong Kong, the sights, sounds, and smells of the place seem lesson enough. But most tourists see only the outward symptoms of Hong Kong's prosperity and may not grasp the underlying foundations of its economic policies: private property, the rule of law, limited government, low taxes, balanced budgets, sound money, and sensible regulation.

What are the main features of Hong Kong's economy? First, the Hong Kong government is small and unobtrusive. What it does, it does well. The streets are clean and safe with well-maintained parks. Public schools and hospitals educate and treat millions of residents every year. In land-short Hong Kong, almost half the population lives in government-owned housing or receives housing subsidies. Tap water is safe to drink. Most communicable diseases have been eradicated, and any outbreak is quickly arrested.

To achieve all this, the government requires less than one-fifth of the gross domestic product (an economic measure of any country's output of goods and services). By way of comparison, all levels of government in the United States spend as much as two-fifths of national output, and many countries in Europe spend more than half. Many people who study global public finances generally agree that the public services in Hong Kong are of higher quality than in most big cities around the world.

Think about this from the perspective of the taxpaying residents of Hong Kong. They get to spend four-fifths of what they earn on what they want to buy, do, or see. The government is not engaged in an endless grab for the taxpayer's money to pay for more and more programs that people do not want in exchange for higher taxes.

Hong Kong has the world's lowest tax rates. Business firms pay 16.5 percent profits tax if incorporated, and 15 percent if unincorporated. Individuals pay a maximum standard rate of 15 percent on salaries. There is no tax on interest earnings, dividends, or capital gains. There are miscellaneous taxes on rental income, hotel accommodations, and frantic betting at Happy Valley and Shatin race courses. Fees and charges—you pay for what you get—are also important sources of revenue. Government provision of water, postal services, and the airport are run on a commercial basis and do not lose money.

Budget deficits, so commonplace in Western democracies, are nowhere to be found in Hong Kong. The government's budget is in surplus nine of every ten years. Accumulated surpluses are so large that the government can pay all its bills for months and months without collecting a penny in new taxes. The Hong Kong government runs its financial affairs better than most private firms, even in Hong Kong.

The Hong Kong dollar is literally as good as the U.S. dollar. Bank notes come in different sizes and colors, with pictures of the Hongkong Bank, Standard Chartered Bank, and the Bank of China on reverse or front sides. But every one of these pieces of paper in circulation is backed by U.S. dollar assets held by the Hong Kong Monetary Authority. The numbers are different because it takes HK$7.80 to buy a greenback. The value of the Hong Kong dollar, at 7.8 to one U.S. dollar, has remained fixed since 1983.

Limited government, low taxes, and sound money are the ingredients of good government. Thomas Jefferson must have had Hong Kong in mind, though it did not yet exist, when he said, "That government is best which governs least." Were he still bolder, he would doubtless have said, "If the government is limited, the people will prosper."

Private Enterprise

Along with free trade, limited government, low taxes, and sound money, the Hong Kong government scrupulously keeps out of private business affairs. The playing field is level as the government gives no subsidies to particular firms, sectors, or individuals. It does not favor importers over exporters; manufacturing over commerce, finance, or construction; management over labor; or labor over business. It does not impose a minimum wage. It neither encourages nor discourages unions. Business license fees are modest and are waived for very small, one-man businesses. The government does not favor Hong Kong citizens over foreign investors, nor does it grant special preference to foreign business. It does not own or operate the bus companies, power companies, the trams, the ferries, cross-harbor tunnels, or the telephone company—all are private, profitable ventures.

Private enterprise on a bedrock of private property and the rule of law are the defining hallmarks of economic life in Hong Kong. Sir Philip Haddon-Cave, Hong Kong's financial secretary during the 1970s, once remarked that "in particular, businessmen in Hong Kong must never be deprived of their sacred right to lose money." His point was that private individuals and firms take the risks of investing money, time, and effort and therefore deserve to keep the fruits of success. When they lose money, it too is their own, not the taxpayer's.

The concept of private property is easy to understand. Individuals, families, or firms own their homes, businesses, machinery, automobiles, antiques, furniture, and a wide variety of financial assets. Stocks, bonds, bank accounts, certificates of deposit, trusts, and other financial assets are registered in the names of individuals, families, or private firms, not in the name of the government. The government does not tell people what to do with their property, to whom they can sell, or at what price. Every individual and firm in Hong Kong is free to buy and sell its property and, if it wishes, ship the funds out of Hong Kong for safe keeping in the Cayman Islands.

The Rule of Law

The rule of law is much harder to understand than private property. It may be possible to buy a house across the border in Shenzhen and secure a deed of title to the property. But if that title should have any encumbrance that the buyer did not know about, resolving a dispute in China will be fraught with difficulty. A bribe is more likely to get the encumbrance removed than a good lawyer.

For most of us, the rule of law has even more basic connotations. If someone does us a wrong, we can seek and obtain redress through the legal system. This is generally not available in China. In relations between individuals and the state, the state all too often simply detains the individual without a hearing and jails him without a trial. In basic commercial transactions, who you know or have paid off is more important than what happened. For instance, in recent years many small Hong Kong investors paid large deposits to "developers" for speculative housing projects in China. The projects were never built, and the investors have no way to recover their money. This could, admittedly, happen anywhere, but in most countries governed by the rule of law, developers do not share their bounty with judges who are likely to hear the case and with politicians who appointed the judges.

The rule of law in Hong Kong is distinct from and contrasts with the rule of man in China. China's history has little experience with constitutions, parliaments, and courts of law. It has much experience with arbitrary autocratic emperors, dictators, warlords, and ruthless Communist Party officials. This difference between Hong Kong and China is so important that it cannot be overstated. Put as bluntly as possible, words about law do not mean the same thing in Chinese as they do in English. There is no common ground for similar understanding of the "rule of law" between Hong Kong and China in the light of their different political histories.

The origins of the rule of law in Britain and the United States are more than a thousand years old. Their roots lie in the common law, the Magna Carta, medieval charters, Parliament, independent courts, John Locke's *Second Treatise on Government,* and constitutions that protect the rights of individuals from the depredations of government. It is exactly the other way around in China. There the law serves the interests of the state against individuals. Individuals had, and still have, no rights, God-given or in a state of nature. In matters of law, guilt, not innocence, is presumed, and courts serve the state, rather than restrain it. This gap in meaning is so wide that it cannot be bridged until China becomes a Western democracy.

The Chinese constitution has gone through five major revisions. No matter. The words do not mean what they say, at least not when read in English translation. Chinese citizens are granted rights of free expression, but are locked up if they speak freely. They enjoy every other right that appears in any Western country's bill of rights or constitution—unless, that is, they try to exercise them. Chinese citizens are often locked up without reason and released without reason. When China's National People's Congress enacts a Basic Law for Hong Kong that includes guarantees of civil liberties, it does not mean in the Western sense that there really is a basic law for Hong Kong that secures the blessings of liberty for the people of Hong Kong.

A good example of the application of "the law" in China is the case of Australian citizen and businessman James Peng. Mr. Peng had textile and property interests in Shenzhen and became embroiled in a dispute with Shenzhen authorities in 1993 over the control of his interests. The Shenzhen government demanded that he turn over a large share of his company to them. Failing to reach a satisfactory resolution, he sought the assistance of Ding Peng, the niece of Deng Xiaoping, in May 1993. Her response, in a turn of fate, was to transfer 52 percent of the company to herself and her partners and state-owned companies and to arrange for Mr. Peng to be jailed. Mr. Peng won a civil lawsuit against Ms. Ding preventing her from taking over the company, but Chinese officials ignored the court order.

Mr. Peng was then taken from his room at the Mandarin Hotel in Macao on 13 October 1993 by the Macao police and delivered across the border to Chinese police. During the next two years, Shenzhen prosecutors tried, and failed, several times to convict Mr. Peng on a variety of charges. He was not permitted bail during that time. On 28 September 1995 a Chinese court finally convicted Mr. Peng of corruption and embezzlement and sentenced him to eighteen years in prison and deportation. His specific crime was a violation of an amendment to China's company law that was enacted more than a year after his arrest—an *ex post facto* law. According to the account of this affair that appeared in the 29 September 1995 issue of *The New York Times,* no evidence was offered in court to substantiate the charges. Since 1991, the Hong Kong government has had to lobby for the release of eighteen other businessmen who had been detained without trial in southern China. Peng's case and others illustrate the arbitrariness of what passes for "Chinese law" and point out the dangers of crossing politically powerful officials.

Words have meaning, at least in the West. The word *liberty* means freedom from unjust or undue government control. It does not mean any such thing in Chinese, nor has it ever meant any such thing through all of Chinese history. The word did not exist in China until the nineteenth century. The Chinese word for liberty, *ziyou,* was manufactured by combining two existing Chinese ideographs to represent the Western word. But there was no basis in China's linguistic or political heritage to capture the notion of the rights of individuals to be secured against the power of the state. The meaning assigned to *ziyou* in a Chinese dictionary bears no resemblance to the meaning assigned to *liberty* in any American or British dictionary of the English language.

In Chinese, the Western concept of liberty as inhering in the rights of individuals is construed as anarchy, loose grains of sand that fall through a person's hand. Anarchy in Chinese lore is a great political misfortune. Order is the supreme virtue. Individuals expressing their own views and doing their own thing upset the Confucian scheme of personal and social relationships. They also upset Communist Party control of China's vast masses of people.

Liberty, *ziyou,* is also synonymous with bourgeois liberalism, the great class enemy of socialism and the proletariat. The day before tanks and troops fired on thousands of unarmed students in Tiananmen Square, a large white banner with five characters appeared from a hotel window: *fan dui zi you hua.* It means "oppose bourgeois liberalism." Liberty, *ziyou,* left unchecked, posed a great threat to the communist rulers of China. They could not, and still cannot, tolerate in their midst a "goddess of democracy," certainly not one modeled after the "statue of [bourgeois] liberty."

Until the nineteenth century, the Chinese language did not contain any words for privacy, nor did emperors or communist officials ever respect individual privacy. In China, a man's home was not and is not his castle. Today, China's leaders are rushing headlong to create civil, commercial, and criminal legal codes, which require wholesale importation of Western legal precepts and expertise. But the Communist Party never hesitates to do what it wants, regardless of what any of the old or new laws say.

Hong Kong's social, economic, and political future is defined by two documents. The first is an international treaty known as the Joint Declaration, signed by China and Britain in 1984. This document says that Hong Kong can remain autonomous for fifty years after 1997, save in matters of security and diplomacy. The second is the Basic Law, enacted in 1990 in Beijing by a rubber-stamp legislature, which is supposed to serve as Hong Kong's "mini-constitution." Both documents are full of words that seem to ensure all the liberties that 6 million residents of Hong Kong enjoyed under British rule.

In chapter 4, we examine in more detail the language of Hong Kong's constitutional framework. Here we want to make the point that the rule of law, along with low taxes, limited government, sound money, and letting people take their chances in life's economic arena, are the keys to Hong Kong's prosperity.

Liberty and the rule of law go well beyond the right to make money. Other freedoms may be more important. These include religious freedom, freedom of speech, freedom of assembly, a free press, and academic freedom. Churches, newspapers, and universities in Hong Kong are free in word and deed. Religious freedom does not hang on the colonial governor's whim to permit or suppress the right to worship in accord with personal belief. A free press does not hang on some censor's whim. Academic freedom is not bound by the need to obey a political overlord, and citizens can march in the streets, present petitions to Government House, and hold political rallies.

Hong Kong residents can form political parties, run for office, and even criticize the most senior government officials—and need not fear a midnight knock on the door. Hong Kong residents do not worry about being sent to reform camps in the distant Chinese countryside.

Hong Kong is free to be Western or Chinese, as its people see fit. Chinese culture is alive and well in Hong Kong, along with the best of the West. There is no official culture, religion, beliefs—what the communists call "class consciousness"—that Hong Kong residents must respect.

Hong Kong's 6 million Chinese differ from their mainland cousins in the most fundamental way: they are free. John Locke may have been just another *gwailo* when he wrote the great political discourse on private property in 1690, but every Hong Kong Chinese shares the freedom of his bequest.

Prosperity

Freedom is the true source of Hong Kong's vitality, and its fruits are found in every aspect of life. When tourists leave Hong Kong, they take home stuffed suitcases and shopping bags, but also strong memories of the sights and sounds of millions of hard-working Chinese buying, selling, trading, and just plain making money—and getting to keep most of it.

To the *Guinness Book of Records.* Keep in mind that Hong Kong's population just barely exceeds 6 million people, compared with more than 250 million in the United States and 1.2 billion in China.

- ☐ The port of Hong Kong is the world's busiest container port. It handles more containers than the whole of Britain, and ranks third behind the United States and Japan in annual container throughput. Hong Kong exports more containers in one month than Australia in an entire year, and each year the port expands by building new capacity equal to a port the size of Oakland.
- ☐ Hong Kong is the world's eighth-largest trading entity in terms of the value of its merchandise trade, rising from tenth place in 1993. Total exports and imports exceed $250 billion, twice as large as its gross domestic product. The territory is the world's eleventh-largest exporter of services.
- ☐ Hong Kong has the second-largest stock market in Asia outside Japan and the sixth-largest overall in the world.
- ☐ The presence of more than 80 of the world's top 100 banks makes Hong Kong a world-class international financial center. The external assets of its banking sector rank fourth in the world, and foreign exchange turnover places Hong Kong sixth in the world.
- ☐ The Chinese Gold and Silver Exchange Society operates one of the largest gold bullion markets in the world.
- ☐ Per capita income exceeds $25,000, placing Hong Kong in the top ten countries in the world.
- ☐ Hong Kong ranks sixth-highest in the world in terms of household spending power.
- ☐ Reflecting global demand for scarce office space, Hong Kong was the most expensive business location in the world in 1995, topping $150 per square foot per year in prime locations.
- ☐ Foreign currency assets of the Exchange Fund exceed $50 billion. Per capita, Hong Kong ranks second in the world after Singapore.
- ☐ When the new airport is operational in 1998 at Chek Lap Kok, a two-deck Lantau fixed crossing, carrying a railway as well as roads, will constitute the Tsing Ma suspension bridge linking Tsing Yi Island to Ma Wan. The bridge will be the world's longest span, 1.4 kilometers carrying both road and railway, and its concrete towers will be 206 meters tall, as high as some of the tallest office buildings in Central District.
- ☐ The Tian Tan Buddha at the Po Lin Monastery on Lantau Island is the largest outdoor bronze statue of Buddha in the world.
- ☐ Hong Kong has Southeast Asia's largest oceanarium.
- ☐ Hong Kong is Asia's most popular travel destination.

☐ During 1993, Hong Kong became the first major city in the world to have a completely digital telecommunications network. It has the second-highest rate of mobile phone use in the world, and per capita, the greatest number of paging subscribers and the second-largest number of fax machines.

☐ Hong Kong publishers print about 80 daily newspapers and more than 600 periodicals.

☐ Life expectancy is 81 years for women and 75 for men; infant mortality is 5 per 1,000 live births.

☐ Hong Kong residents rank first in the world in consumption of expensive brandy.

Hong Kong is the leading financial, industrial, trading, and communications center of Asia and is a world leader in many areas. More than any other place in the world, Hong Kong embodies the American dream—the opportunity for anyone to get rich. Indeed, according to *Forbes,* Hong Kong has two of the world's top ten billionaires, and several more among the top 100 or 400 richest people in the world.

We have presented a panorama of Hong Kong. The impressions are clear, crisp, and unmistakable. Hong Kong's free economy has served the 6 million people who live there, as well as millions of people in China and thousands of businessmen from around the world. It has done so in a tiny, crowded, resourceless granite outcropping on the southeast coast of China. It has an excellent harbor, to be sure, and a hard-working people born of a tradition of study, thrift, and commercial adventure. If those are universal Chinese traits, then why are most of China's 1.2 billion people poor? After all, they are keen to study, save, and invest. It is just that their communist masters have not allowed them the freedom to prosper. Indeed, China is the only country in the world where the majority of Chinese are poor.

In the next segment, we trace the historical context of Hong Kong's remarkable achievements.

In the Context of History

Britain formally occupied Hong Kong Island on 26 January 1841. The British were seeking a secure base from which to conduct trade with China because they disliked the conditions under which Chinese officials confined them to the factory area on Shamien Island in the midst of Canton. British traders were forbidden to enter the city or learn the Chinese language and were not permitted year-round residence.

Misunderstandings and differences of opinion led to the first of several Opium Wars. This is not the place to rehash those stories. For our purposes, it is sufficient to note that China ceded Hong Kong Island to Britain under the Convention of Chuenpi, signed on 20 January 1841.

Fewer than 6,000 people occupied Hong Kong Island when the British ran up the Union Jack for the first time. In June 1841 Captain Charles Elliot held the first land auction. All land belonged to the Crown, but the principle of allocating land to private individuals and firms to the highest bidder set the economic tone for Hong Kong. Almost the very first transaction ensured that a scarce resource, land, went to its highest-valued use—to whomever paid the most for it.

Within months Elliot gave way to Sir Henry Pottinger, who initiated further hostilities resulting in another treaty, the Treaty of Nanking, which was ratified in June 1843, thereby securing British occupation *in perpetuity*.

A second altercation, again arising from misunderstandings, was resolved in 1860 by the Convention of Peking. The treaty gave Britain a *perpetual* lease to the southern tip of the Kowloon peninsula as far as Boundary Street, including Stonecutters Island.

As other European countries demanded, and received, concessions from China, Britain extracted additional territory from China. In 1898 Britain acquired the "New Territories," which constituted the area north of Kowloon up to the Shenzhen River and 235 islands. The acquisition of the New Territories took a different route: instead of cession in perpetuity, China granted a *ninety-nine year lease*. A ninety-nine year lease would certainly create a legal problem in 1997, but that must have seemed an eternity to the colonial authorities, none of whom is alive to day.

Foreign rule in Hong Kong was surely noxious to every Chinese subject in Hong Kong because Chinese tradition placed a great virtue on the superior status of rule by the Confucian-trained leaders of the "middle kingdom." Few expected that citizens of the middle kingdom would choose to live under a foreign flag. How wrong those skeptics were! By 1851, almost 31,000 people made their home in Hong Kong; only 1,500 were not Chinese. Eighty years later, Hong Kong numbered 879,000 souls and all but 19,500 were Chinese.

Why were the skeptics confounded? Liberal British rule proved irresistible to the mercantile-minded Chinese. Nineteenth-century Britain was the world's leading proponent of free trade, and that policy was put in place in Hong Kong. Laissez-faire defined Hong Kong as a market where all were free to come and go, buy and sell, without fear or favor. The government defined property rights, enforced the law, and judged all subjects impartially.

How far did laissez-faire extend? Hong Kong's first city hall, which was built by public subscription, was a magnificent two-story building that housed a museum, public library, and a theater. It became a community cultural center for concerts, lectures, and numerous social functions. (The old Bank of China Building, next to the Norman Foster, see-through Hongkong Bank at No. 1 Queen's Road Central, now sits on its site.)

Chinese emperors and their mandarins oppressed the masses of Chinese with heavy, burdensome taxes. Mid-nineteenth-century Hong Kong was almost completely free of taxes. As an economist might remark, the relative price of living in Hong Kong compared with China was irresistible, even if one had to live under the political rule of "barbarians."

Hong Kong gradually entered the modern age. By the Chinese revolution of 1911, Hong Kong had gas, the Peak Tram, electricity, electric tramways, a railway, public education, and a university, and a series of reclamations pushed the waterfront out into the harbor.

From its beginning, Hong Kong developed as an entrepôt free port —as a mart and storehouse for goods in transit to Asia and the West. After World War II, entrepôt activity diminished when the transition to an industrial economy took place. Export-oriented light industry, augmented by banking, insurance, and shipping services, was the mainstay of Hong Kong's economy. In keeping with its free-port tradition, Hong Kong imposed no tariffs or other restrictions on the import of commercial goods.

Hong Kong's postwar transformation was so dramatic that it absorbed a doubling of its population between 1938 and 1956. Refugees arrived from Shanghai, bringing capital and entrepreneurial skill, while Chinese immigrants from the south supplied labor for the factories. In recent years, the factories have given way to a burgeoning service sector.

Hong Kong became the goose that laid golden eggs. Everyone made money—the locals, expatriates, and China too. King Midas, not King George or Queen Elizabeth, should have adorned the dollar bills issued by the government of Hong Kong. But the policy of laissez-faire that had defined its politics for so long dissipated in the late 1970s. Hong Kong's saving grace had been rule by an efficient, benign colonial government over a passive people grateful for freedom and the opportunity to make money. China, too, had been on live-and-let-live terms with Hong Kong because mainland leaders derived enormous benefit from the conversion of the barren rock into a veritable gold mine under British administration.

Hear no evil, see no evil, speak no evil had worked wonders for decades, but investors and markets cannot stand uncertainty. As the 1980s approached, the comfortable colonial arrangements gave way to increasing anxiety among international and domestic investors over the future of Hong Kong. Would banks give long-term mortgages with no guarantee of contracts being enforced after 1 July 1997? Would the shrinking time horizon of British rule constrict investment and the future growth of the economy?

Books about the future of Hong Kong could fill a small library: *City on the Rocks, The Betrayal of Hong Kong, The End of Hong Kong, The Fate of Hong Kong, The Fall of Hong Kong, The Future of Hong Kong, A Date with Fate, Hong Kong in Transition, Hong Kong Prepares for 1997, Hong Kong and 1997, Hong Kong's Transition to 1997, Countdown to 1997, Hong Kong Countdown, Democracy Shelved, Hong Kong: In Search of a Future, Hong Kong 1997,* and *A Borrowed Place: The History of Hong Kong.* These books describe in fine detail the visits to Beijing of Sir Murray MacLehose, governor of Hong Kong, Humphrey Atkins, minister of state at the Foreign and Commonwealth Office, and Prime Minister Margaret Thatcher. Mrs. Thatcher insisted on the validity of all three treaties ceding and leasing the various components of Hong Kong to Britain. Deng Xiaoping, China's paramount leader, stated unequivocally that China would assert its sovereign right to all of Hong Kong by 1 July 1997.

Between 1982 and 1984, Hong Kong was in crisis. Tax rates were increased to cover unprecedented budget deficits, land values collapsed, the stock market declined, the currency came under pressure, and real investment fell 8 percent, declining for the first time in postwar history. Jardine, Matheson and Company, Hong Kong's premier trading firm, which is synonymous with the colony's foundation and history, announced it was moving its legal registration to Bermuda. Immigration lawyers from the United States, Canada, Australia, and Britain set up shop in Hong Kong in response to the interest of many Hong Kong residents to emigrate.

Change is always frightening, but the magnitude of impending change was horrifying. A colonial administration restrained by the oldest elected parliament in the world would be replaced by a ruthless dictatorship. Chairman Mao, in one fanatical political campaign after another, had killed millions of his own people. More than stability and prosperity were at stake in Hong Kong. The communists had never shown any tolerance for bourgeois liberty or Western civil rights and political freedoms. All of a sudden, the *gwailos* who held high rungs in Hong Kong's civil service seemed downright attractive.

Ensuring the Future

What could be done to ensure Hong Kong's future before 1997 and especially after China took over? For their part, China's leaders repeated
again and again: "Trust us." "Investors should put their hearts at ease."
"We have no intention of changing the status quo." "We will not interfere in Hong Kong's internal affairs." "You can keep your present way of
life, including economic and personal freedoms." "You can retain your
capitalist system for at least fifty years after 1997." "We've issued ten
points that guarantee that Hong Kong people will run Hong Kong with
autonomy." "Hong Kong people can have two passports." "Land leases
will be extended after 1997 with cheap premiums." "Hong Kong's exports quotas would be kept separate from those of China." And so on.
Indeed, China seemed to wage an all-out war of promises to reassure
Hong Kong's people and international investors that life after 1997
would remain largely as before.

China promised to give Hong Kong specific constitutional status as
a special administrative region (SAR) of China in accordance with Article 31 of the fifth revision of China's constitution. Deng Xiaoping, as
Chinese leaders are wont to do, coined the phrase *one country, two systems*. Chinese would recover sovereignty and have authority over defense
and foreign affairs, but otherwise let Hong Kong maintain economic, social, and political systems that differ from China.

If China's leaders are honorable men, why was the future of Hong
Kong so contentious? One reason is that China's own constitution bears
little resemblance to actual conditions in China. Its people have never enjoyed the freedoms spelled out in any of the ever-changing Chinese constitutions. China's post-1949 constitutional promises have not been
worth the paper they are printed on, and this reality does not instill confidence among Hong Kong's people.

Using the issue of the validity of leases in the New Territories after
1997, Britain raised the issue of Hong Kong's future with Chinese leaders. Fresh from its triumph in the Falklands, Britain initially held out for
the letter of the 1843 and 1860 treaties that ceded Hong Kong Island
and Kowloon in *perpetuity*. China, holding all the trump cards, said no,
and Britain ultimately conceded the point. Then Britain held out for
some kind of continuing administrative link with Hong Kong after 1997;
her majesty's representatives argued that a continued British presence
would build confidence. Again China said no. (You may wish to read our
1985 book to see why China had its way in these negotiations.)

What was left for Britain to gain from the negotiations? It had lost
face to the point of complete humiliation. In a spirit of reconciliation,

China could magnanimously restore British face by signing a document that guaranteed, line by line, Hong Kong's rights and privileges after 1997. Britain could then present to its colonial subjects in Hong Kong a bona fide international treaty that would be registered at the United Nations by both the British and Chinese governments.

On 19 December 1984, in Beijing, the prime ministers of the two countries signed a Joint Declaration. Britain promised to restore Hong Kong to China, while China declared its "one country, two systems" policy for Hong Kong. The Joint Declaration provides the following:

☐ Hong Kong will enjoy a high degree of autonomy. Socialist policies in the mainland will not be applied in Hong Kong, and Hong Kong will maintain its capitalist system and way of life for fifty years after 1997.
☐ The people of Hong Kong will continue to enjoy their rights and freedoms under Hong Kong law.
☐ Hong Kong will retain its common-law system, and a court of final appeal will be established in Hong Kong.
☐ Hong Kong will retain its free-port status and separate customs status.
☐ Hong Kong will have autonomy in economic, financial, and monetary fields. There will be no exchange control, and the Hong Kong dollar will be a freely convertible currency. China will not levy taxes on Hong Kong people.
☐ Hong Kong will determine its own shipping and air agreements.
☐ Hong Kong people will retain their land rights up to 2047.
☐ Hong Kong people will retain right of free entry to and departure from Hong Kong.

Several annexes elaborated these policies; provided for a Joint Liaison Group which would resolve issues up to the year 2000 but which would not interfere in the remaining years of British administration; explained the status of residents who were British Dependent Territories Citizens after 1997; and addressed land leases and rights.

Paragraph 3 (12) of the Joint Declaration stated that the policies of China regarding Hong Kong were to be stipulated in a Basic Law enacted by the Chinese National People's Congress. The drafting process began in 1985 and ended five years later when the Basic Law was promulgated on 4 April 1990. This process, too, was contentious, and it remains the subject of much analysis and criticism. But the document itself reads as a very generous grant of rights, more so than the Magna Carta or even the U.S. Constitution, because it includes an "economic bill of rights." And since Hong Kong's business community is reputed to be more concerned with making money than with civil rights, an entire section of economic guarantees represents an extraordinary concession on China's part. Imagine: One of the world's most ruthless communist regimes has promulgated the only list of economic rights and guarantees in any constitution anywhere in the world, even if it applies only to the Hong Kong SAR.

Nevertheless, it is a mistake to equate these rights with freedoms. In the Anglo-American tradition, rights and liberties inhere in individuals, not in the state. In the Chinese tradition, rights are grants of the state —given to and taken back from individuals at the whim of the state, with or without cause.

So the future of Hong Kong was settled. Derek Davies, the editor of the *Far Eastern Economic Review*, wrote a glowing story in 1984, attacking nay-sayers and critics with hammer and tong, and others chimed in their approval. Property and stock prices took off, investment capital poured into Hong Kong, the local currency became as good as the greenback, and Hong Kong investors seized the opportunity to participate in China's own economic reforms. With the exception of a short-lived setback from Tiananmen Square in June 1989, Hong Kong went from strength to strength. Indeed, China replaced the United States as Hong Kong's largest foreign investor by 1994. Chinese enterprises poured billions of dollars into Hong Kong properties and equities and bought up or into thousands of local firms.

Things were not so rosy as we finished our analysis in 1995. The economy flourished until mid-1994, after which disturbing symptoms began to appear—falling stock and property values, a slowdown in business incorporations, a pullback in personal consumption, and rising unemployment, to name a few. Rents for spacious residential apartments in the prestigious mid-level area of Hong Kong Island fell by as much as half between 1994 and 1996, while the unemployment rate reached an eleven-year high of 3.5 percent. China has interfered in Hong Kong's internal affairs so much, despite the Joint Declaration's stipulation that it would not, that the dictionary needs a new entry under *autonomy*. China has broken so many promises to the British, the Hong Kong government, and the people of Hong Kong that the word *promise* must have in Chinese eyes an expiration date short of five, much less fifty, years. Hundreds of thousands of Hong Kong's people have emigrated, and expatriate police officers have resigned in droves. More than half of Hong Kong's listed companies are domiciled outside Hong Kong; the vast majority are registered in the British Crown Colony of Bermuda, which rejected in August 1995, by three to one, a referendum on independence.

Hongkong and Shanghai Banking Corporation, the colony's preeminent financial institution, shifted its legal domicile to Britain. Xu Jiatun, China's representative in Hong Kong for seven years, lives in exile in Los Angeles. A great cloud of uncertainty hangs over Hong Kong.

❋ 3 ❋

The Sweet and Sour of China

Since 1980, China has stood in first place on almost every global economic indicator. Its economy has grown at 9 percent a year for seventeen years. Its coastal provinces, especially those near Hong Kong, Macao, and Taiwan, have grown even faster. What were rice fields a mere decade ago are now full-blown cities. Modern industrial parks have sprung up like weeds. China has several fully electronic stock exchanges. In the month of June 1995 alone, the number of cellular phone customers shot up by 746,000. China's businessmen run multinational enterprises. Billions of dollars in foreign investment pour in, and trade surpluses are in the tens of billions of dollars. Hunger and famine have largely disappeared. Chinese infrastructure is expanding so rapidly that many of the world's largest construction projects are in China. Some of its people are growing rich, heeding the maxim of China's paramount leader, Deng Xiaoping, that "to get rich is glorious."

Despite the progress, most Chinese remain dirt poor. The majority scratch out a living in the countryside even as visitors to Canton and Shanghai witness an economic boom. Still, the gulf between Hong Kong and even the most prosperous parts of China remains as large as the gulf that separated Shanghai from the rest of China during the first half of this century.

The Chinese people are studious, hard-working, thrifty, loyal, and devoted to family—they possess, in short, all the traits that should make a people succeed. And succeed they have, but until recently not in China. Overseas Chinese are the driving force of economic development in Thailand, Malaysia, Indonesia, and the Philippines. Overseas Chinese thrive in the West Indies, the United States, Canada, Australia, Britain, and other Western democracies. Overseas Chinese have turned Singapore, Taiwan, and Hong Kong into economic powerhouses. Per capita income in Singapore and Hong Kong has surpassed many European nations, and Taiwan is fast catching up.

China's economic story fills two chapters. The first is that of Mao Zedong and his revolutionary cadres who survived the "long march" into the caves of Yenan in the 1930s. Mao was a zealous Marxist revolutionary. After seizing power in 1949, he sought the overthrow of all existing social, political, and economic institutions in order to fashion a new society. His new China would be free of private property, exploitation, and class conflict and would achieve a great egalitarian revolution. With him in charge, every Chinese person would work for the noble cause of socialism, building a strong, independent China.

To that end, Mao engaged in endless class struggle. He even turned on his own Communist Party when necessary, using his young Red Guards to root out bureaucratic elements that opposed his policies. He sought to weed out all those who fit his definitions of reactionary, counterrevolutionary, landlord, and member of the national and petit bourgeoisie classes. All who opposed Mao met a tragic fate.

Within seven years, Mao had nationalized the entire economy, even small shops and handicraftsmen. What little private sector there was in 1949 had completely disappeared by 1956. Not content, he embarked on a Great Leap Forward and then collectivized the countryside. Both programs failed disastrously. Nevertheless, by 1960, the state or the Communist Party ran the entire economy.

Throughout Mao's rule, China was in turmoil and its economy stagnated. Mao followed the Soviet model of state-owned heavy industry but changed course when necessary to survive. In a last desperate effort to create the socialist China he craved, he launched the Great Proletarian Cultural Revolution. He shut down the schools and sent millions of Red Guards throughout the country to terrorize their elders in every sphere of life. Finally, the madness ended, leaving China in tatters.

Deng Xiaoping picked up the pieces. Although a stalwart Communist Party member, he was a pragmatist in economic matters and is known for his saying that "it doesn't matter if a cat is black or white as long as it catches mice." He launched a series of economic reforms, calling them "socialism with Chinese characteristics." A better name would have been "China with capitalist characteristics." He opened China's economy to the West and established special economic zones along the coast that enjoyed a large measure of economic freedom. He completely overhauled the agricultural sector, creating free markets virtually overnight. He has tried to transform state-owned industry, but has not been very successful. Deng and his colleagues are not prepared to face tens of millions of unemployed urban workers who would lose their jobs if inefficient state-run industries were shut down.

Deng has done everything in his power to put China's economy in the major leagues. He has welcomed billions of dollars of foreign investment from compatriots in Hong Kong, Taiwan, and Southeast Asia. He has returned confiscated property to its former owners. He has allowed a great deal of economic experimentation in the special coastal zones and has permitted regional officials to offer investment and production incentives to foreigners and residents. He has presided over the largest tax cut in world history—the share of total tax revenues in China fell from 31.2 percent of the gross domestic product in 1978 to a meager 9.1 percent in 1994, a stunning 71 percent reduction in the total tax burden.

While Deng went to market, he did not become a democrat. He was less autocratic than Mao, but only because he had to depend on the support of his colleagues. Mao, like President Abraham Lincoln, could poll his cabinet and do exactly the opposite of what it unanimously voted. Deng had to get support from a majority of the Communist Party's inner circle. But Deng never sanctioned political liberalism, or *ziyouhua*. When Li Peng issued the order to open fire at Tiananmen Square, he had Deng's approval.

From time to time, elements in China tried to slow economic reform, fearing that a market economy would pose a high risk to Communist Party rule. Deng fought off his opponents in a race for growth, sometimes succeeding, sometimes failing. Several of the reform documents approved by the National People's Congress during the 1980s sound as if they were cribbed from Adam Smith's *Wealth of Nations*.

It is this spectacular economic story that gave, and still gives, hope to many in Hong Kong that China will honor its promises to Hong Kong. It makes no sense to kill the goose that lays golden eggs.

A Transformed Economy

Facts and figures show how far China has come under Deng's leadership. A visitor to Hong Kong and Canton in 1949 would have found few differences in the standard of living. Both cities were drab and their residents were poor. Per capita income was under $100 in Canton and not much higher in Hong Kong. When Deng took power in 1978, per capita income in China had reached $200, whereas it had reached $3,670 in Hong Kong, more than eighteen times higher. Thirty years of economic chaos under Mao left China a Third World country.

Deng believed that a strong economy was necessary to restore China to its glorious past as a great power. He saw that Park Chung-hee in Korea, Chiang Ching-kuo in Taiwan, and Lee Kuan-yew in Singapore had succeeded brilliantly. None of his successful neighbors practiced multiparty democracy. Their recipe was firm political control tied to free-market policies. They showed that China could become rich yet remain firmly under the control of an authoritarian regime.

Deng worked miracles. Between 1978 and 1992, China's gross domestic product (GDP) grew from 3.59 billion yuan to 24.02 billion yuan. (The yuan—or renminbi—is China's currency, or dollar, which trades in the range of eight to the U.S. dollar.) The output of primary industry —agriculture, fishing, mining—increased nearly sixfold. Industrial output rose eightfold. When inflation is removed from these numbers, China's GDP increased 233 percent.

Average annual growth of GDP was 9 percent, and of industry about 10 percent. Economic growth since 1992 has hummed along at 10 percent each year. In the special coastal zones, annual growth has run about 20 percent, which means that the output of the zones doubles every four years.

The World Bank and other international institutions have adopted a new measure of national wealth, known as purchasing power parity. In China, for example, many goods and services are cheaper than in the United States. This means that the same amount of money buys more in China. On this measure, China ranks third in world purchasing power, just behind Japan. Its national purchasing power is 35 percent that of the United States. In per capita terms, China's purchasing power parity measure in 1993 was $2,040, in comparison with $22,200 in the United States.

Using more traditional measures of GDP at current exchange rates, China does not fare so well. It falls to tenth place, with total output one-twelfth that of the United States. China's per capita income on this method was $370 in 1993.

Other indicators reveal strong growth. From 1986 to 1993, coal output rose 27 percent and electricity output 77 percent. There were major gains in natural gas, crude petroleum, natural rubber, iron ore, and steel output. Textile production shot up 30 percent, synthetic rubber and cement production doubled, and automobile tire output tripled. The annual and monthly statistical bulletins issued in China are packed with numbers of economic expansion in all sectors of the economy.

The country's balance sheet looks much healthier in the mid-1990s than when Deng took over. China's international reserves grew more than fivefold, from $11 billion in 1986 to surpass $60 billion in 1995. This reflects a huge growth in foreign trade. Exports quadrupled from 108 billion yuan in 1986 to 426 billion yuan in 1993. Indeed, China's huge trade surplus with the United States is a serious bone of contention between the two countries and threatens to exceed the large U.S. trade deficit with Japan.

The number of telephones nearly doubled from 1990 to 1995, and long-distance lines more than doubled. Much of Hong Kong's backroom processing, including directory assistance services of the Hong Kong Telephone Company, is located in south China. Guangdong Province, adjacent to Hong Kong, has grown so much that its residents have as many telephones as Beijing and Shanghai combined, which are China's political and commercial centers. A housing boom, financed by rising incomes, has more than doubled per capita living space from about 8 to 17 square meters from 1978 to 1990.

Deng radically transformed the structure of China's economy in the short span of fifteen years. Agriculture functions as an essentially free market in which remuneration is linked to output. The more you produce, the more money you make. The comprehensive system of state ownership of industry has given way to a mixed system of state-owned, collective, individual, and foreign-funded enterprises. The unitary, highly centralized planning structure was converted into a decentralized market system. Monetary, technological, labor, real estate, information, and other production markets have developed.

Deng began his economic reforms in 1978. Unlike Mao, who changed economic policies every few years, Deng stayed the course. Farmers were given something akin to private property rights on the land they tilled. For the first time in modern China, a growing number of seemingly private or semiprivate businessmen could actually plan ahead for more than a few days at a time. The managers of special economic zones were free to experiment with various economic incentives to lure investment from Taiwan and Hong Kong, and they succeeded brilliantly.

The atmosphere in Hong Kong grew euphoric during the 1980s as millions of Chinese told each other and foreigners willing to listen that Deng's new China was different. Many prominent residents of Hong Kong who had suffered under Mao placed their faith in Deng's promise of "one country, two systems." Unfortunately, Deng's reforms came to a momentary standstill on 4 June 1989 in Tiananmen Square, dashing the hopes of Hong Kong's people.

But Deng stayed his economic course, and the economic fallout from Tiananmen quickly dissipated. Indeed, Hong Kong underwent its most dramatic boom in history. Property and stock prices spiraled upward as Hong Kong became the main economic base from which foreign and domestic investors participated in China's spectacular growth. But even as Hong Kong and China prospered from each other, the dispute over Hong Kong's political future grew ever more contentious.

During the early 1990s, concerns about the economic future of Hong Kong seemed to disappear off the radar screen. The two economies of Hong Kong and neighboring Guangdong Province were becoming so integrated that economic convergence was proclaimed as a matter of fact. Around this time, economists, ignoring the political realities, began to refer to China, Hong Kong, and Taiwan as a single entity— Greater China. Hong Kong manufacturers hired several times more workers across the border than in Hong Kong. The Hong Kong dollar freely circulated throughout Guangdong Province. Cross-border traffic jams were commonplace.

As Hong Kong businessmen moved into China, more than a thousand Chinese firms and tens of thousands of mainland residents moved into Hong Kong. The Bank of China commissioned world-renowned architect I.M. Pei to design its Hong Kong headquarters—a most spectacular, albeit controversial, landmark. Mainland firms bought into such well-established Hong Kong firms as the territory's flagship carrier, Cathay Pacific Airways. George Shen, editor in chief of the Chinese language *Hong Kong Economic Journal,* quantified the remarkable increase in mainland China's business involvement in Hong Kong. China became the leading foreign investor in Hong Kong, surpassing the United States and Japan. China's investment in Hong Kong–listed companies is in the tens of billions of dollars, the assets of its banks in Hong Kong have risen as high as $100 billion, and numerous Chinese state enterprises list their shares on the Hong Kong Stock Exchange. National, provincial, and municipal-level mainland companies in Hong Kong are engaged in a wide variety of activities, encompassing manufacturing, construction, and real estate management, importing and exporting, transportation and tourism, finance and insurance, and property investment. More and more mandarin, or putonghua, is heard on the streets, reflecting growing numbers of mainlanders. Money changers buy and sell the renminbi, China's national currency, on every street corner.

Political Reforms in Hong Kong

The economic union of Hong Kong and China served Deng's interests. But Deng wanted no part of Western bourgeois liberalism. That, however, is exactly what he got.

On 9 April 1992 the Conservative Party won reelection in Britain. Prime Minister John Major then replaced Sinologist and Foreign Office diplomat David Wilson as governor of Hong Kong with former MP Chris Patten, a career Tory politician. As Wilson departed Hong Kong, he warned Patten that public disputes with China would not serve the interests of Hong Kong. But Wilson was in Major's disfavor, so he spoke to deaf ears.

Six months later, in October 1992, Patten made his first policy statement on the colony's *political* institutions: "Democracy is not destabilizing. It helps to make communities more prosperous. It helps to make a government better too."

Alarm bells went off in Beijing and Hong Kong. Overnight, the smooth transition from British to Chinese sovereignty and administration over Hong Kong became turbulent. China's insistence that Hong Kong's internal political development converge with its plans for the territory's future was challenged by Patten, who unveiled proposals for more representative government. For 150 years, Hong Kong had been ruled by benign colonial bureaucrats, whose policy decisions were ratified by a compliant, appointed Legislative Council. Now the British government, with Patten as its instrument, rushed to build stronger democratic institutions in Hong Kong before 1997.

Chinese officials in Beijing and Hong Kong immediately denounced Patten for failing to consult China. Despite vociferous Chinese opposition, initial polls showed that a majority of Hong Kong residents overwhelmingly supported Patten's proposals for greater democracy.

Hong Kong was split. In one camp were the democrats, led by Martin Lee, who overwhelmingly supported Patten's call for democratic reform. Indeed, for the democrats, the reforms were too little, too late. In the other camp was the pro-Chinese business community, which feared that political disputes with China would destabilize the economy. One Chinese official after another warned that China might not honor the 1984 Joint Declaration if Patten persisted with his reform proposals. China accused Britain of violating the Joint Declaration, the Basic Law, and other Sino-British agreements and understandings. Chinese officials warned Britain not to proceed with building a new airport without gaining mainland approval.

For a while, the bloom faded off the rose. The stock market dropped 1,000 points in four days, the new airport and container terminal were put on hold, and other long-term investments became questionable. China threatened to suspend future meetings of the Joint Liaison Group, a joint body of British and Chinese officials, which had been created by the Joint Declaration to oversee transition issues. China said that all contracts, leases, and agreements signed or certified by the Hong Kong government without China's approval would be invalid after 1997. China also threatened to dismantle all political structures in 1997.

In February 1993, following high-level meetings of top Chinese officials in Canton, and as Patten recuperated from heart surgery, China threatened to set up a second "stove" or shadow government in clear violation of the Joint Declaration that accorded Britain full responsibility for the administration of Hong Kong until 30 June 1997. The second stove would take the form of a consultative committee of prominent, pro-China Hong Kong residents. Meanwhile, the Legislative Council did not flinch. It approved bills to lower the voting age to eighteen and make voting methods more democratic, despite strong words from China. Patten's critics accused him of throwing Hong Kong into turmoil for the sole purpose of securing an honorable British retreat in 1997.

As the dispute dragged on, China appointed another group of advisers, consisting of pro-China Hong Kong conservatives who emphasized stability and prosperity over more democracy. This group included several members of the Legislative Council and several prominent academics.

The controversy continued unabated. Other issues about Hong Kong's future came into the open. One Hong Kong journalist was given a draconian sentence in China for what amounted to everyday, ordinary reporting of economic facts in Western countries. Several China-watching magazines closed their doors. Hong Kong collectors worried about the status of their antiques, and some moved their treasures abroad for safe keeping. The director of the China State Council's Hong Kong and Macao Affairs Office, Lu Ping, visited Hong Kong for eight days in May 1994 to celebrate the Bank of China's inaugural issue of local banknotes. He refused to meet with Governor Chris Patten. When he finally spoke in public, he issued a stern warning to local prodemocracy politicians that China would not tolerate anyone using Hong Kong to influence Chinese politics. Local television showed Lu inspecting Chinese army units that were to be stationed in Hong Kong after 1997.

Finally, on 30 June 1994, exactly three years before the handover of Hong Kong, the Legislative Council approved Patten's political reforms. The vote was a surprising 32–24, given outspoken opposition from China. The reforms substantially broadened the franchise for so-called functional constituencies (professional groups), increased the number of directly elected seats, and replaced the remaining appointed members with representatives of the colony's elected District Boards. General elections were scheduled for September 1995. Political reform, at least in the short run, became a certainty.

China's response? In early September its parliament, the National People's Congress, passed a unanimous resolution to abolish the political structure based on Patten's electoral reform package. To repeat, the vote was unanimous—not a single dissent. Political continuity, expressed in the concept of the "through train" on which the members of Hong Kong's Legislative Council elected in 1995 would remain in office until the next scheduled elections in 1997, ceased.

In November 1994 China broached the idea of a "provisional" legislature, one that would hold sway from 1 July 1997, when China would dissolve the existing political institutions, until new elections were held in 1999. Its tasks would be to enact those laws that no freely elected legislature in Hong Kong would pass. It would dismantle the political reforms, restructure the electoral system to favor pro-China parties, repeal or amend a bill of rights approved by Hong Kong's colonial legislature, and enact laws on treason, secession, sedition, subversion against the Central People's Government, or theft of state secrets that are acceptable to their patrons. Fears were expressed that this provisional body would be handpicked by China. Such a provisional entity has no legal basis in the Basic Law.

Disputes continued into 1995, centered on Hong Kong's court of final appeal, or supreme court. China was in no mood to tolerate any British or Hong Kong criticism. It effectively dictated the terms of a Sino-British agreement. The court would be established only after the transfer of Hong Kong to Chinese rule. It would have no say over "acts of state." China indicated that the court might be restricted to the adjudication of economic disputes and that its decisions might be reviewed by a still higher body in China.

After the initial shock in 1992, when the markets were in turmoil, Hong Kong's economy seemed unperturbed by China's ceaseless name-calling of Patten. The Hang Seng index on the Hong Kong Stock Exchange reached the dizzying height of 12,000 in mid-1994. Property prices rose without interruption, as even occupants of tiny flats became U.S. dollar millionaires. Rental values in Hong Kong's central business district made it the world's most expensive office accommodation. Thousands of Hong Kong residents who had gone abroad to acquire foreign papers returned to live and work in Hong Kong. The entire episode of democratic reform seemed to be nothing more than a tempest in a teacup—at least from a narrowly economic point of view. Money was to be made, and was being made, on all sides.

The summer of 1994 marked something of a turning point. From a high of 12,000, the key Hang Seng index fell below 9,000 by the following summer. Commercial rentals fell about a third. Residential rentals fell by as much as half in the upper-income market. Personal savings increased, while the purchase of consumer durables and revenues of fancy restaurants declined. In August 1995 Moody's Investors Service issued a warning that the future Hong Kong dollar's link to its U.S. counterpart might be at risk due to possible capital flight, reinforcing the controversy kindled by Nobel laureate Milton Friedman's identical warning several months before. The Hong Kong dollar instantly weakened, and local banks immediately raised overnight interest rates to alleviate pressure on the local currency. The government indicated that it was not going to implement the third and fourth phases of a four-stage banking reform to deregulate interest rates because of concern over stability of the territory's financial system in the remaining time before 1997. Unemployment reached an eleven-year record high, exceeding the rate following the Tiananmen incident. Estimates of unemployment among real estate agents and car salesmen ran as high as 25 percent. The secretary for financial services, Michael Cartland, stated that "the banking system is sound, but with the operating environment becoming more difficult, it's sensible not to do anything to add to the problem." Hong Kong was beginning to show its nervousness with less than two years of British rule remaining.

Summary

Let us summarize the story. Since 1978, starting from a very low base, China has enjoyed sustained high growth. The fruits of that growth are evident in the big cities and the coastal provinces. The policies that Deng followed to attain high growth consisted largely of removing the shackles of a textbook communist command-and-control economic system from more than a billion people. Given ever-increasing bits of economic freedom, China's enterprising people produced ever-larger output of goods and services.

But it would be wrong to equate gradual relaxation of Communist Party control over economic matters, and the China it has wrought, with the fundamental institutions of a free society that underpin Hong Kong —private property, the rule of law, limited government. China still lacks well-defined property rights. To all intents and purposes, there is no "rule of law" in China. And its government and the ruling Communist Party are far from limited in their exercise of power. Hong Kong remains as different from China as meat and potatoes are from fish and rice.

To make matters worse, China's leaders deeply distrust Britain and its liberal, democratic supporters in Hong Kong. China's leaders remain obsessed with righting the historical wrong of colonial occupation of sacred Chinese soil. And, given the socialist prism through which they see Hong Kong, they really do not understand what makes Hong Kong work. They even believe they can run Hong Kong better than the British. The facts are beside the point when China's leaders ground their approach to Hong Kong on the basis of "class standpoint."

It takes a long time for a dedicated Chinese communist official to understand Hong Kong. And it has happened only on very rare occasions. The best example is Xu Jiatun, who served as head of Xinhua (New China News Agency), China's unofficial consulate, in Hong Kong during much of the 1980s. During his tenure, Xu faithfully reflected the party line in all disputes with the Hong Kong government. But gradually Xu came to understand Hong Kong in institutional terms of private property, the rule of law, and limited government—that these were the factors underpinning Hong Kong's success. His eyes, as it were, opened. Xu ultimately published an article that tried to direct the attention of China's leaders to what he had learned about Hong Kong.

Where is Xu today? He lives in Los Angeles, perhaps in voluntary exile. He has not returned to China since taking up residence in the United States. Why did China's leading spokesman in Hong Kong during the 1980s abandon his compatriots in both Hong Kong and China? Xu has never spoken in public about his decision.

In the Context of History

There is little in China's history that provides its leaders with a basis for understanding Hong Kong. Private property, the rule of law, and limited government evolved over centuries of intellectual and institutional ferment in Britain and the United States. To give but one example, as late as 1831 only one in twelve adult males was eligible to vote in British parliamentary elections, and Britain still does not have a written constitution. It took a long time for the concept of individual rights and limited government to materialize in the British and American governments.

These concepts have never existed in China. From its founding some four millennia ago until 1911, China exhibited great political continuity. Dynasties came and went, but the imperial system remained intact. An emperor reigned supreme. He was bound by custom, not by law, subject only to the Confucian precept of governing by moral authority. Moral authority is a poor substitute for the "rule of law," especially when a specific emperor is disinclined to take his Confucian responsibilities to heart. Sometimes an emperor adhered to the Confucian analects. Sometimes, not. The structure of authority ran from the top down. The emperor ruled and the people obeyed. The Chinese people had no say in the choice of their ruler or government except to rebel or revolt. But the leader of the revolt simply became the new emperor, and nothing else changed. Political parties and elections, the stuff of democracy, were unknown in Chinese politics.

The Confucian imperial scheme created and solidified a class structure that put scholar-administrators in command, followed in descending class status by soldier, peasant, and handicraftsman. This framework provided centuries of social stability. It emphasized the obligations of those who were ruled. Nowhere in the centuries of Oriental despotism did rights and privileges emerge in Chinese political thought or practice.

The Qing Dynasty, China's last, collapsed under the pressures of Western intrusion and social change. Under the leadership of Sun Yat-sen, who tried to graft the Western values of democracy and equality as well as modern economic concepts onto Chinese culture in his great work, *The Three Principles of the People,* patriotic Chinese overthrew the remnants of the Manchu Qing Dynasty, which had ruled since 1644. They proclaimed the formation of a new Republic of China on 10 October 1911 and imported an American legal scholar to help draft its first constitution. But old practices died slowly.

Sun Yat-sen was elected president of the provisional government but resigned on 1 April 1912 in favor of General Yuan Shi-kai, who was considered the most likely person to work out an early abdication of the Qing monarch. Yuan, however, took advantage of his presidency to enlarge his sphere of influence. He purged the government of members of Sun's Kuomintang (Nationalist) party, dissolved the legislature, hand-picked his own lawmaking body, and promulgated a new constitution that gave himself despotic powers comparable to those of former emperors. He proclaimed 1916 the first year of a new dynastic cycle. Unfortunately for Yuan, he died in misery and disgrace in June 1916, and China lapsed into warlordism.

It is not easy to impose a Western constitution on an autocratic system. The attempt failed under Sun Yat-sen. It failed under Chiang Kai-shek. It never got off the ground under Communist Party rule, from Mao Zedong through Deng Xiaoping. The essence of constitutional government is that individuals have rights and that governments are limited —this is the basis of Hong Kong. The essence of Chinese political history is that governments or ruling political parties are unlimited and that individuals have no rights.

Hong Kong differs from China as day from night. Chinese leaders are informed by Chinese history, culture, language, and tradition. China, as its name in Chinese characters signifies, is "the middle kingdom." All others are outsiders, barbarians, or foreign devils; in a word, inferior. It would take a heroic repudiation of history and communist ideology for any Chinese leader to understand Hong Kong, much less regard the colony's institutions as preferable to those of China. Xu Jiatun, perhaps alone, made that leap. But it took him seven years, and Hong Kong does not have another seven years left under British rule.

What did Xu Jiatun learn from his years in Hong Kong? He came to understand the importance of private property and the "rule of law."

These two institutions, which developed over the centuries, figuratively "tie the hands" of politicians. Like the subjects they govern, politicians are bound to obey the law, rather than use or abuse it for personal or partisan gain. Is it likely that Jiang Zemin, Li Peng, Zhu Rongji, the top generals of the People's Liberation Army, and other prominent leaders of China will accept the judgments of Hong Kong courts that run counter to their interests? The remainder of this book answers this question. Alas, the answer is, "no!"

❋ 4 ❋

Words Have Meaning,
or Do They?

As British rule comes to an end, the locus of power shifts to Beijing, Canton, Shanghai, and other regions of China. After 1997, the future of Hong Kong will be determined by the future of China, which is spelled out in chapter 5.

The story line is simple. Profound uncertainty and turmoil in China will destabilize Hong Kong's market-driven economy. Every economic indicator will oscillate, sometimes wildly. Stock prices and property values will rise and fall like a yo-yo. Any positive statement by a leading Chinese official will restore confidence; any negative statement will shatter it. Without giving away the details of China's tumultuous morrow, the mainland will undergo political, social, and economic upheaval. The transition will not be a simple transfer of power to a new generation. Instead, it will be the equivalent of a dynastic upheaval—a wrenching transformation—and Hong Kong's six million people will not be immune to the fallout. The new Hong Kong Special Administrative Region, or HKSAR as it will be known formally, will mimic its new master. Its government, its economy, and its social fabric will be buffeted first one way, then the other.

The optimists, the pro-China crowd in Hong Kong, argue passionately that China will not kill the goose that lays the golden eggs—at least not knowingly or willingly. Why, they ask, would China shoot itself in the foot? Chinese firms, belonging to the state, the military, and semiprivate enterprises, have invested billions of dollars in Hong Kong and would incur substantial losses in any economic downturn. Given that China values Hong Kong's investments in its booming southern provinces, it has little incentive to shut off the inflow of capital and technology. Moreover, the Communist Party wants to lure Taiwan back into its fold, using the "one country, two systems" Hong Kong formula. Why would the party set back the cause of reunification by bungling its take-over of Hong Kong? Each of these arguments makes sense. But posing them runs into a semantic question of huge proportions: do these words mean the same thing to the leaders of China as they mean to Western observers?

The optimists say that China has gone the extra mile to ensure the future of Hong Kong. China has made solemn promises in the Joint Dec-laration, an international treaty registered with the United Nations, that shows honor-bound intent. China has enacted a constitution for Hong Kong, the Basic Law, which guarantees political, social, and economic rights for its people. Why go to such trouble if its purpose is to fool everyone? China could have shut off the flow of water to Hong Kong any time during the past few years—and it did not. China could have in-terfered with the flow of people and commerce across its border with Hong Kong—and it did not. The optimists find in China's words and deeds proof of good intentions to honor the Joint Declaration and Basic Law.

The pessimists, the prodemocracy crowd in Hong Kong, point to an equally long list of episodes of betrayal. Despite a clause in the Joint Declaration stating that "the Government of the United Kingdom will be responsible for the administration of Hong Kong" until 30 June 1997, China has repeatedly interfered in the internal affairs of Hong Kong. China blocked a new airport project for years in opposition to Governor Chris Patten's proposals to expand democracy. China stalled an expan-sion of container port facilities. It set up a "Preliminary Working Com-mittee" of notables that resembles a shadow government in Hong Kong. China announced plans to dissolve Hong Kong's legislature on 1 July 1997 in protest of a vote by it to expand local democracy.

Mao's Legacy

Mao Zedong has been dead for a long time. What has he got to do with the future of Hong Kong? The answer is, "a lot." Mao's credentials in-clude many important achievements: founding member of the Chinese Communist Party; revolutionary leader; hero of the Chinese civil war; first leader of the People's Republic of China; architect of China's eco-nomic policies during its first quarter century; and prolific author.

Among Mao's writings are three of special importance: "On Prac-tice," "On Contradiction," and "Combat Liberalism." He wrote them between July and September 1937 when he and his comrades were holed up in the caves in Yenan. Footnotes cite the works of Vladimir I. Lenin and Friedrich Engels on the law of contradiction, the most basic law of dialectical materialism (fashioned by Engels and Karl Marx, authors of *The Communist Manifesto*).

The core principle of dialectical materialism is that contradictory, mutually exclusive, opposite tendencies exist in all phenomena and processes of nature, including the mind and society. As we said earlier, Aristotle would find this metaphysical formulation illogical. Mao built his entire framework for political education and action on this platform. Nowhere does he cite Adam Smith, John Locke, David Hume, Thomas Jefferson, or James Madison.

"Combat Liberalism" is only three pages long. In it, Mao defines liberalism, or *ziyouzhuyi*, which translates literally as "freedom-ism" or "liberty-ism." The key word in the phrase is *ziyou*, freedom. Viewers of CNN may recall that "oppose liberalism" was the party's rallying cry when it sent troops and tanks against unarmed students in Tiananmen Square.

What does Mao say in "Combat Liberalism?" He writes that "we advocate an active ideological struggle, because it is the weapon for achieving solidarity within the Party." In contrast, "liberalism negates ideological struggle." Mao is especially eager to warn his comrades that liberalism has no place in the communist movement.

"Liberalism stems from the selfishness of the petty bourgeoisie, which puts personal interests foremost. . . . Liberalism is a manifestation of opportunism and conflicts fundamentally with Marxism . . ." (emphasis added). Therefore, "all loyal, honest, active and staunch Communists must unite to oppose liberal tendencies."

Hong Kong's economy, society, and lifestyle epitomize liberalism. Hong Kong may well be the world's premier "liberal" society. Even though Mao's essay will be sixty years old in 1997, it was a good indicator of China's behavior at Tiananmen Square. As long as the Communist Party remains China's supreme authority, Mao will remain relevant.

The other two essays require more study. "On Practice" is the more important of the two pieces. It is subtitled "On the Relation between Knowledge and Practice—Between Knowing and Doing." Mao wrote it to educate party members on the Marxist conception of "truth."

The core principle is that knowledge becomes verified only in the process of social practice. There is no such thing as purely abstract or theoretical knowledge. But practice is not a matter of personal choice. It is restricted to *class struggle*. As Mao says, Marxist philosophy, that is, dialectical materialism, has two characteristics: "one is its class nature, its open declaration that *dialectical materialism is in the service of the proletariat;* the other is ... its emphasis on practice as the foundation of theory which in turn serves practice."

To continue: "perceptual knowledge turns into logical knowledge through the complex and regularly recurrent practices of production and *class struggle* of man in society." Mao attributes the genius of Marx, Engels, Lenin, and Stalin to their personal participation in class struggle. Marxism-Leninism is true, says Mao, because it was verified in the subsequent revolutionary class struggle. The communists, in other words, won.

If all this sounds confusing to you, it should; it sounds just as confusing to us. We will try to translate it into English. Mao, speaking for the Chinese Communist Party, vanguard of the proletariat and its leading element, proclaims that *logic and evidence are to be used in the service of the proletariat, not the bourgeoisie.* This formulation requires selective use of logic and evidence (in the normal sense of the words) by party members. Whenever the revolution and class struggle are served by logic and evidence, then by all means use them. If, however, the opponents of revolution and class struggle use logic and evidence in the service of the bourgeoisie, indeed the exact same logic and evidence used by communists to advance class struggle, then party members must reject that specific use of logic and evidence. In Mao-think, logic and evidence are not really logic and evidence under circumstances that favor the bourgeoisie.

To repeat, logic and evidence are relative to time and place—the service of the proletariat as determined by the Communist Party, but especially by its leader, Mao Zedong.

Let's try to explain this one more time. Truth is when Mao finds it useful to use logic and evidence to advance class struggle, the revolution, and secure power for himself and the Communist Party. As conditions change during these struggles, so too does truth. Today's truth becomes tomorrow's lie if the opponents of class struggle seize on the same logic and evidence. If truth derives from logic and evidence, then truth is relative to time and place—to whatever serves the proletariat.

It may seem to Western minds that Mao is just changing his mind, saying one thing today and another tomorrow. But such perception misses the central point of Marxism-Leninism-Maoism. Truth is defined in terms of class struggle, revolution, and advancing socialism, whatever may be in vogue at the time. Each time Mao changed his mind on how to serve best the proletariat, truth changed.

Are you bewildered? Does this sound nonsensical to you? It should. Marxism is a contradiction. It is a framework for reason that is inherently illogical most of the time, nonlogical at other times, and occasionally logical (in Aristotelian terms) at other times. It is logical in the Western dictionary definition of "logic" when being logical serves the proletariat—as Mao thinks appropriate. It is also a recipe for saying and doing whatever you want, if you have the power to execute your commands or your opponents. Marxism-Maoism legitimizes any and every word or deed, as long as you stay in charge.

At this point, let's stop talking about the proletariat and simply talk about the Communist Party. During Mao's life, the "great helmsman" and the party were one. When he spoke, the party spoke. When he issued orders, the party acted. What happened to the proletariat, you may ask? Were its interests well served? In the view of Mao and most communists, the proletariat lacked sufficient class consciousness of what it meant to be the proletariat. Therefore, the Communist Party had the right to run everything. This sounds like a justification for the exercise of unbridled power.

One last translation before moving on to Deng Xiaoping, China's paramount leader after Mao. Cutting through the Marxist double talk, Mao says basically this: When it serves your interest, make promises. When it serves your interest, break promises. Breaking promises is not lying—at least not in a Marxist communist vision. Breaking promises is simply the application of logic and evidence that leads to a new truth, one applicable to the current conditions of class struggle.

As to the written and spoken words that define the content of those promises, their meaning changes as circumstances warrant. The meaning depends on the nature of the class struggle at any moment in time. Accordingly, Chinese dictionaries are revised whenever it is necessary to include new ideological formulations or change old ones. China's constitution, in this spirit, has undergone five comprehensive revisions in less than fifty years, reflecting the shifting currents of political definitions.

What does class struggle in the service of the proletariat mean for Hong Kong? Class struggle means that supporters of China should oppose British colonialism, and oppose the bourgeoisie or big capital. Class struggle may also mean that supporters of China should unite with Hong Kong's bourgeoisie in joint struggle against the British colonialists. Or, if need be, class struggle may even permit good communists to work with the British to advance the development of socialism in China.

It's a very small stretch to go from constantly changing conditions of class struggle, which define the truthful use of logic and evidence, to *lying*. It really is all right to *lie* in the service of the proletariat, if that is how the party believes class struggle can be advanced.

Hong Kong's 6 million Chinese residents are well advised to read "On Practice," "On Contradiction," and "Combat Liberalism" in full. It would be premature, at least before 1997, to dismiss these essays as old hat.

"Economics Takes Command"

We saw in chapter 3 the new China. Since Deng's accession to power in the late 1970s, China's economy has led the world in growth. Private firms, along with town and village enterprises, are rapidly displacing some of the dodo birds of state-owned enterprise. Foreign trade runs in the tens of billions of dollars. Chinese travel to Hong Kong and abroad by the thousands. The People's Liberation Army is as much a for-profit business association as it is a military organization. "To get rich is glorious." The sons and daughters of Communist Party elders, the princelings, run business conglomerates with substantial overseas holdings.

Indeed, Chinese firms now have more capital invested in Hong Kong than do American or British firms. They own substantial stakes in Hong Kong blue chip companies. They list their own shares, known as "red chips," on the Hong Kong Stock Exchange. They own factories, apartments, wholesale firms, retail firms, restaurants, tour operators, shipping companies—the list goes on. For example, the president of CITIC, China International Trust and Investment Corporation, earned $25 million in 1994 and owns mansions around the world.

In reverse, Hong Kong capital is the direct cause of prosperity in Shenzhen and Guangdong Province. Hong Kong businessmen employ a mere 500,000 factory workers in Hong Kong, but more than 3 million in south China. Hong Kong has become a high-tech service center for south China. The economies of Hong Kong and south China are so integrated that their separation is now inconceivable.

To many leading businessmen in Hong Kong, the economic future of Hong Kong is no longer an issue. Hong Kong depends on south China and south China depends on Hong Kong. In their view of things, Deng Xiaoping is only paying lip service to the rhetoric of Marxism-Leninism-Mao Zedong thought, updated with his own thoughts. That lip service, they maintain, is designed for domestic consumption in China to retain legitimacy for the Communist Party. After all, Deng has led the effort to build a real "state" that is distinct from the party, with codes of commercial, civil, and criminal law. He has led the effort to establish a real judiciary. He has led the effort to develop the "socialist market economy," with the emphasis on "market."

It is too late to turn back the clock. China is committed, unalterably, to economic policies that promote prosperity. Turning the old Marxist slogan that "Politics takes command" upside down, in China today "Economics takes command."

Deng really is different from Mao. Or is he? And how about his successor, or successors? How many affluent Hong Kong residents are prepared to leave their money and families in Hong Kong when both might be safely ensconced overseas?

Deng has said that he wants to live to see 1 July 1997. On that day of national pride, China will rectify the humiliation inflicted on all patriotic Chinese when Li Hung-chang signed Chinese territory over to Britain in the late nineteenth century. Deng has called the shots on Hong Kong since the late 1970s, when the future of Hong Kong became a salient issue to Britain and China.

On closer scrutiny, Deng is not the capitalist he is often made out to be. A civil libertarian he most definitely is not. He has never hesitated to take measures to jail dissidents or punish opponents of his policies, inside or outside the Communist Party. Whenever he has had to choose between party or state, he invariably comes down on the side of the party.

Deng is not the autocrat that Mao was. He has had to balance different interests, sometimes veering left, sometimes right. He has been unable, for example, to shut down inefficient, money-losing, obsolete state industries. He has not built independent state institutions that can reject party imperatives. Regarding Hong Kong, he has fiercely resisted any expansion of democracy. His emissaries have called Chris Patten "prostitute," "criminal," and worse.

The Legal Issues

Let us examine the future "legal structure" of Hong Kong as spelled out in the Joint Declaration, the Basic Law of Hong Kong, and the Constitution of the People's Republic of China. The balance of this chapter is a lawyer's brief on Hong Kong.

We start with the Joint Declaration (appendix A). It is a short document, only slightly more than 1,100 words. It includes three annexes and two memoranda, which total another 8,000 words. The declaration stipulates that China will resume sovereignty on 1 July 1997 but gives Britain responsibility for Hong Kong until that moment. It commits China and Britain to cooperate during the transition from 1984 to 1997, establishes a Sino-British Joint Liaison Group to work on transition issues, and deals with land leases.

Shortly we take up the issue of sovereignty, and what the Chinese conception of it means for Hong Kong. To get back to specifics, the Joint Declaration transfers 6 million people who have been living an increasingly good life in a largely free society to the goodwill of another. That "another" is the People's Republic of China. This transfer is almost unprecedented. It is a mirror image of the collapse of the Berlin Wall and the Iron Curtain. China, to put it mildly, is a whole lot less free than

Hong Kong. China's citizens have been victims of their own government on more than one occasion. And worse, the prospects of serious political disruption are on the immediate horizon.

The Joint Declaration is a treaty between two sovereign states under international law and is registered with the United Nations under Article 102 of its charter. Its provisions are thus binding in international law, both before and after July 1997, at least according to the British House of Commons.

What does the declaration's treaty status mean in practice? Can disputes over it be adjudicated in the International Court of Justice? The answer is, "not really."

International law is a law principally of states. For the court to hear any case arising from the Joint Declaration, both parties must agree to refer the matter to the court, or have previously consented to have all their legal disputes referred to it. There are no statements in the Joint Declaration to bring future disagreements to the court. Moreover, China has not accepted the "compulsory jurisdiction" of the court. Therefore, neither the British nor any other nation can drag China before the court for failing to abide by the terms and conditions of the declaration.

In the event of a breach, claimed or real, of the Joint Declaration, the parties are limited to seeking consultation between themselves. Neither Britain nor China can compel the other to adhere to its terms. This limitation is primarily a British problem. Once sovereignty is formally transferred in 1997, the British will have no mechanism to enforce any of its provisions.

Here is China's concept of sovereignty as expressed in its legal journals: Sovereignty is "the supreme power of a state to decide independently its internal and external affairs in accordance with its own will." This explains the oft-stated Chinese response to such Western complaints of human rights violations and copyright infringements. The West must not interfere in China's internal affairs, which are within its sovereign rights. China has already warned the international community that it would not tolerate criticism of its handling of Hong Kong matters after 1997, as such matters would be internal affairs. China is prepared to reject any efforts to internationalize Hong Kong.

In point of fact, China never acceded to the notion that sovereignty over Hong Kong was vested in the British Crown. In the Chinese view, sovereignty is vested in a single state. It is indivisible. Even to acknowledge its divisibility would serve as a basis to justify the "carving up" of China by the capitalist-bourgeois European powers in the nineteenth century.

China's view of sovereignty means that its control over the internal affairs of Hong Kong cannot be subordinate to the will of any other state. Sovereignty is not negotiable and is unlimited.

The Basic Law, Hong Kong's "mini-constitution," is not an international treaty. Instead, it is a law, a simple statute, enacted on 4 April 1990 by the National People's Congress of China. That congress, for most of its history, has been a rubber-stamp body, uniformly and often unanimously approving the policies of China's party or state leaders.

On 28 June 1990 the Standing Committee of the National People's Congress issued a decision stating that the English translation of the Basic Law had been finalized upon review by the Law Committee of the National People's Congress and that the English text shall be used in parallel with the Chinese text. *In case of discrepancy between the two texts in the implications of any words used, the Chinese text shall prevail.* This decision gave full authority to mainland officials to interpret the meaning of the Basic Law. This was a change in policy from the text of the Joint Declaration, signed in 1984, which states that both the English and Chinese texts shall be equally authentic.

Regardless of linguistic semantics, it is important to understand the status of a law. It is valid only until replaced, or amended, by another law. It is not the same thing as a constitutional measure, which requires, in most countries, a much more complicated procedure to reverse or change. To change a law requires only a simple majority vote in the National People's Congress. This has never been a tough proposition.

Some might argue that the Basic Law has semiconstitutional status because it was enacted as a statute under the provisions of Article 31 of China's own constitution of 1982. But this is stretching the meaning of constitutional status. Hong Kong's Basic Law is not on the same footing as China's constitution. It is dependent on it in subordinate fashion. It cannot survive if the National People's Congress votes to repeal Article 31, revise Article 31, or enact a new statute to replace the existing Basic Law. The viability of the Basic Law is subject to Chinese whim.

What is the relationship between the Central People's Government of China and Hong Kong? China's constitution states that the central government has supreme authority under its provisions. Laws, statutes, rules, and regulations issued by state bodies are next in order of authority. Then follow local regulations and municipal ordinances. The hierarchy is strictly defined so that laws of a lower level cannot contravene those of a higher level. These general provisions would be true, of course, in any country governed by the rule of law where words have meaning.

In concrete terms, lower levels of government, such as the new Hong Kong Special Administrative Region (HKSAR), cannot contravene China's constitution or its national laws. In application, the Standing Committee of the National People's Congress is empowered to reject any law enacted in Hong Kong that it believes does not conform with the Basic Law or the relationship between the central authorities and the region.

The story is not so simple as all this sounds. Article 5 of China's constitution stipulates that the basis of the socialist economic system in China is public ownership of the means of production. Yet the Joint Declaration and Basic Law state that Hong Kong can practice its capitalist system for fifty years after 1997. The problem is that there is no specific provision in China's 1982 constitution that says that the central government can exempt Hong Kong, or any region for that matter, from the national constitution.

In the United States, where courts have power of judicial review, such bizarre legislation would probably be declared unconstitutional on the grounds that exempting one unit of the country violates an explicit provision of the national constitution. It would be as if the equal protection clause of the U.S. Constitution, the Fourteenth Amendment, did not apply to Mississippi, thereby permitting the Mississippi state legislature to impose slavery in that state if it so chose. Of course, such an exemption would be patently absurd.

Chinese courts do not have power of judicial review. Indeed, in the "politics takes command" mode of Chinese national life, political imperatives often dictate judicial and legal outcomes. Therefore, Hong Kong's legal position within China is tenuous at best. In point of fact, the Basic Law drafting committee specifically rejected a proposal to modify China's constitution to conform with the Basic Law.

The present Chinese leadership is perfectly happy to tolerate these obvious inconsistencies between their national constitution and Hong Kong's Basic Law. But this toleration is a matter of policy only, and policies are easy to change. What guarantees or recourse does Hong Kong have should future Chinese leaders decide that the Basic Law violates China's constitution? To which independent court would Hong Kong plead its case? To the standing committee of the National People's Congress?

To summarize, a domestic law, the status of Hong Kong's Basic Law in China, is not the same thing as an international treaty. But the Basic Law had to conform to the Joint Declaration, which appears to be such a treaty, albeit an unenforceable one. Any repudiation or alteration of the declaration would violate an international treaty. Nevertheless, how closely the Basic Law conforms to the Joint Declaration is not subject to legal review. Its conformity is the sole prerogative of China's government or the party leaders who guide it.

The Future Hong Kong Government

It is conceivable, but not likely, that China might scrap the Basic Law altogether before 1997. Therefore, it is worth taking a look at the construction of Hong Kong's government starting 1 July 1997. Bear in mind that China's legislature has voted to dissolve Hong Kong's current legislature on that date, when a new transitional body will be appointed pending the first round of post-1997 elections. Bear in mind, too, that the British role in Hong Kong has been winding down since 1984, so that almost no expatriates remain in high positions.

THE EXECUTIVE

In broad terms, the Joint Declaration and its companion document, the Basic Law, envisage an executive-led government in Hong Kong, coupled with a weak legislature and limited democratic representation. There are no immediate plans for one-man, one-vote direct election of all legislators on the basis of universal suffrage. Nor are there plans for direct election of the chief executive. Hong Kong's new government, as set forth in the Joint Declaration, appears remarkably similar to the colonial structure it replaces—but with one striking difference. Under British rule, a largely disinterested colonial power some 6,000 miles away, restrained by Parliament and a system of common law more than a thousand years old, rarely used the authoritarian powers vested in the documents, the *Letters Patent* and *Royal Instructions,* which provided the constitutional underpinnings of Hong Kong. The new sovereign, China, is much closer, just across the border from Hong Kong, and has a history of ruthlessness against its own citizens. Or, to put it in more straightforward language, Britain governed Hong Kong under the "rule of law," while the Communist Party has run China under the "rule of man."

Under colonial rule, the governor was the kingpin of the system. He represented the British Crown, chaired the policymaking Executive Council, presided over the lawmaking Legislative Council, had the power of pardon, and so forth. The Basic Law gives corresponding power to the chief executive of the newly constituted Hong Kong Special Administrative Region. The chief executive must be a Chinese citizen with no foreign right of abode; he cannot have dual citizenship, a "green card," or a foreign passport. The Basic Law says nothing about the status of his spouse or children. He shall have resided in Hong Kong as a permanent resident for a continuous period of twenty years. He shall serve a term of five years and be accountable both to the central government in Beijing and Hong Kong in accordance with the provisions of the Basic Law.

Ideally, as in any representative system of government, the chief executive should represent the population at large. Most presidents, prime ministers, or chancellors in representative democracies are selected by direct or indirect election of the public. This is not so in Hong Kong.

The National People's Congress in Beijing has enacted a separate law for the formation of the first post-1997 government in Hong Kong. Bear in mind that China's legislature can repeal or amend this law any time it wants. To continue, a 400-member selection committee—100 from the business sector, 100 from the professions, 100 from labor and other grass-roots sectors, and 100 from various Hong Kong political representatives to national Chinese bodies—will appoint the first chief executive. How is unclear. The law says "either following local consultations or by nomination and election following consultation." The law does not set out the committee's procedure. Nor does it say if the ultimate decision on the method of selection is to be determined within the committee, or by the National People's Congress (or whoever tells it what to do). Is there any doubt that China's leaders will make the initial appointment?

Indeed, vagueness suits China's leaders. It allows them to interpret the language of any law or even constitutional provision to serve their specific interests, whatever they may be. Vagueness also blends nicely with the muddled, contradictory framework of Marxist thought that informs Chinese political thinking.

What about subsequent chief executives, those selected after 2002? The Basic Law stipulates an 800-member committee, with 200 from each of the four categories used in the initial selection process. These "electors" are to be picked within Hong Kong by a process "in accordance with the principles of democracy and openness." The ultimate aim, the height of democratic rhetoric, under Article 45 of the Basic Law is the selection of a chief executive on the basis of universal suffrage—after a broadly representative nominating committee makes its recommendation. What if that committee proposes only one name? In any case, the utopian vision of a democratically chosen chief executive, at least in the Western notion of democracy, is not scheduled until 2012 at the earliest, the fifteenth year of Chinese sovereignty.

China's concept of the principle of democracy, as seen in its practice for almost fifty years, bears no resemblance to any Western industrial democracy. The Communist Party is completely dominant, with minor parties permitted to exist only for show. Candidates are invariably handpicked by party leaders or limited to a preapproved list. The closest approximation to Western notions of democracy in China is the one-party tradition that once existed in several southern U.S. states where, typically, whoever won the Democratic Party's nomination was a sure winner in the general election.

THE LEGISLATURE

The second branch of government is the legislature. The Joint Declaration and Basic Law provide for a legislature in Hong Kong. Non-Chinese residents may sit in that body, but their members may not exceed 20 percent of the total. Although the long-term goal is selection by universal suffrage, the immediate post-1997 legislature will be anything but freely chosen by Hong Kong's adult population.

The Basic Law enumerates the usual list of powers and functions. But the document also severely restricts the Hong Kong legislature. No member may introduce a bill that relates to public spending or the political structure and operation of the territory's government. No bill relating to government policies may be introduced without the chief executive's prior written consent, which means without China's prior consent. On its face, the description of the new legislature sounds very much like the colonial Legislative Council—except that the implications of Chinese sovereignty are enormous.

The formation of the first new legislature is a story in itself. It had been hoped that the election of the last Legislative Council under British administration would "ride through" 1997 and become the new special administrative region's first sitting legislature. China's legislature had stipulated that Hong Kong's first legislature after 1997 would have sixty members, no change from current arrangements. Of them, direct election by geographic constituency would pick twenty, functional constituencies (professional, trade, labor, and other activities) would choose thirty, and an election committee the remaining ten. China said that if Hong Kong's last legislature conformed with these arrangements, and if its members pledged their allegiance to the new Basic Law, then the members could retain their seats after 1997—if confirmed by yet another body, a "preparatory committee."

The "through train" derailed in 1994 on Governor Chris Patten's determination to fashion several democratic reforms before 1997. In all, two rounds of reforms lowered the voting age to eighteen; introduced a "single-seat, single-vote" electoral system for all tiers of government —the Legislative Council, District Boards, and Municipal Councils; enlarged the franchise to include more than 2.7 million people from the previously much smaller functional constituencies; and gave the directly elected District Boards the sole say in the election of ten seats. To put these reforms in perspective, in 1981 the electorate numbered a scant 34,381, electing only fifteen officials in all at any level of government.

Remember, the British are supposed to have sole authority to administer Hong Kong through 1997 under the Joint Declaration. So how did China respond? Two months after Hong Kong's Legislative Council approved Patten's reforms, the National People's Congress voted *unanimously* to end Hong Kong's present form of government on 1 July 1997.

China claimed that Patten's reforms violated the Joint Declaration and Basic Law and that it was taking corrective action. It comes as no surprise that China's legislature voted unanimously to undo Patten's achievements on 1 July 1997. China's legislature has a long history of doing the Communist Party's bidding. Besides, the issue of "face" is so important that no Chinese legislator, however resistant to Deng Xiaoping, would take a position endorsing the British colonial governor or his lackeys in Hong Kong.

China moved quickly to fill the new void it had created. Scheduled to establish a "preparatory committee" in 1996, it rushed in December 1994 to set up a "preliminary working committee," a precursor to the "preparatory committee," which would prepare the basis for a provisional legislature. The provisional, temporary body would sit from 1 July 1997 for six months or more until some system of elections would choose a new legislature duly constituted under China's interpretation of the Basic Law. The Basic Law is as flexible as China wants it to be.

A few words on the membership of the "preliminary working committee." It is replete with Hong Kong notables from business, law, and the academy. It even has the anomaly of including members of the colonial Executive Council, who are handpicked by the governor and who are sworn to an absolute oath of secrecy on council deliberations.

THE JUDICIARY

The third branch of government is the judiciary. Under colonial rule, the courts of Hong Kong are independent of the executive and legislative branches. Moreover, their decisions are subject to review and reversal by the Judicial Committee of the Privy Council in Britain. The key point is that the legal system of Hong Kong represents the "rule of law" in the best Western sense of the term. No man is above the law, and the law is applied fairly and impartially—a complete contrast with the legal system in China.

The role and composition of the courts in the new special administrative region have been controversial. One dispute has centered on the number of judges from other common-law jurisdictions that may sit on an appeal panel at any time. The most intense dispute concerns the promised "court of final appeal" that is to replace the Privy Council, an issue that Britain and China settled in the summer of 1995, but a solution vigorously opposed by the bar association of Hong Kong and most of the directly elected legislators.

The language of the Joint Declaration is precise: "The judicial system previously practiced in Hong Kong shall be maintained except for those changes consequent upon the vesting in the courts of the Hong Kong Special Administrative Region of the power of final adjudication." But those words, specifically the official text of the Chinese document, are thin in staying power and flexible in interpretation.

An initial proposal agreed to in secret by the Joint Liaison Group (the body of British and Chinese representatives created by the Joint Declaration to address transition issues) offered a court of final appeal. In it, one judge from another Commonwealth jurisdiction would preside in no more than half of the court's quarterly sittings. In late 1991, in a rare show of independence, Hong Kong's Legislative Council voted 34–11 to reject that approach.

In mid-1995, the issue came to a head. Britain sought to resolve the matter as far in advance of 1997 as possible. Another variation of the previously defeated measure was also rejected by the Legislative Council in early May. Meanwhile, China told Britain that it wanted to limit the role of Hong Kong's court of final appeal—a clear breach of the Joint Declaration—by restricting the court to the adjudication of economic disputes. Political disputes and all constitutional issues would be removed from the court's purview. The Joint Declaration specifically gives such a court the "power of final judgment."

Furthermore, China stated that it might create a supreme body with the power to review the court's decisions, which would augment the existing right of the National People's Congress to have the final say on the interpretation of the Basic Law.

The two governments agreed to a solution in June. China got its way on all issues. In addition, the court is to be established only after the actual transfer of Hong Kong to Chinese rule. The Hong Kong court of final appeal will have no say over "acts of state," which in the common law constitute narrow issues of defense and foreign affairs. Common-law courts hold that no government can invoke "acts of state" against its own citizens. Chinese courts subscribe to no such limits—and may rule that acts of state encompass anything the Communist Party does. There are, of course, no appeals in China against "acts of state." It should be clear that here, as in other aspects of the Joint Declaration and Basic Law, Chinese authorities do what they please.

The unfolding political drama of Hong Kong first requires the selection of a chief executive. Second is the construction of a provisional legislature. Third is the creation of a court of final appeal. These are strange ways to establish "democratic" institutions to ensure a "high degree of autonomy" in Hong Kong. What China says and does is the autonomy Hong Kong will have.

To return to other aspects of the post-1997 legal system, the Basic Law, Article 93, provides for continuity of service of those judges holding office before 1997, with no diminution of compensation and benefits. In late 1994, Lu Ping, the head of China's Hong Kong and Macao Affairs Office, pronounced that the appointment of judges after 1997 would be decided by the executive and legislature of the new government on the advice of a judicial commission. Judicial tenure promised in the Basic Law disappeared in one short breath. The wants ads in the Hong Kong press may have several openings for judges before 1997.

A variety of legal issues cloud the clear application of the "one country, two systems" concept to Hong Kong's legal system. Will the judgments of Hong Kong courts be enforceable in China and those of Chinese courts in Hong Kong? Will Hong Kong courts enforce the judgments of Chinese courts if it is believed or known that political interference affected the decision? In more serious crimes, such as subversion, will local courts be forced to extradite Hong Kong residents to China, which, unlike Hong Kong, has a death penalty. Several businessmen and journalists have received unwarranted prison terms in China. They were presumed guilty, and were found guilty. There is no presumption of innocence in the practical application of Chinese law.

It should be noted that the Basic Law requires that Hong Kong's new legislature enact laws against treason, secession, sedition, and subversion against the Chinese government. The courts of Hong Kong will have no choice but to enforce these laws—laws whose drafters will no doubt require mainland approval.

THE CIVIL SERVICE

The "fourth" branch of government, the civil service, is also structured by the Joint Declaration (Section IV) and Basic Law. Article 101 in the Basic Law stipulates that only Chinese citizens among permanent residents in the HKSAR may fill high-ranking posts of secretaries or heads of departments, and other top positions. British and other foreign nationals may be employed as advisers or may fill professional and technical posts as required.

The case of Haider Barma is instructive. Barma is a native-born Hong Kong resident of Indian heritage, fluent in Cantonese, and a career civil servant with no right of foreign abode. Barma served as secretary of transport in the mid-1990s. He will be forced to give up his job because he is not an ethnic Chinese. This amounts to blatant racism. Many career civil servants, with expertise and knowledge in Hong Kong administrative matters, are taking early retirement, since promotion prospects after 1997 will be based solely on Chinese identity.

HUMAN RIGHTS

Every Western constitution stipulates a list of human rights that are the hallmark of modern, democratic societies. The Joint Declaration does no less, promising freedom of person, of speech, of the press, of association, of travel, and so on. The Basic Law reiterates these personal rights and freedoms, but records, in Article 39, that the "rights and freedoms enjoyed by Hong Kong residents shall not be restricted *unless as prescribed by law.*"

Translation: whatever the new legislature prescribes may restrict the "rights and freedoms" of Hong Kong residents. And the new legislature is certain to do China's bidding.

The Chinese conception of "rights and freedoms" is not grounded in self-evident truths, as the authors of the Declaration of Independence proclaimed. Nor is it grounded in a state of nature, as John Locke supposed. Instead, rights and freedoms are grants of the state, emperor, or Communist Party *that may be restricted by law.* They are not inherent in the individual, to be protected by an independent judiciary whose rulings the executive and legislative authorities will obey. So, for example, the interim legislature that will convene on 1 July 1997 could restrict, by law, many of the rights and freedoms currently enjoyed by the residents of Hong Kong. And law, in China's concept and practice, is not what is meant in the West by the "rule of law." Law, as we have seen in China, is what the party or the state wants to do.

It all boils down to this: who is prepared to trust China's written promises in the Joint Declaration and Basic Law? Evidently not the big business community that has prospered in Hong Kong. The colony's richest man, Li Ka-Shing, has moved his assets offshore. More than half of all listed companies on the Hong Kong Stock Exchange are domiciled overseas, most in Bermuda. From 1984 to 1994, the initial average capitalization of new businesses fell about 40 percent. In 1994, foreign registrations of new business rose 10 percent, while local registrations declined over 30 percent. Even the police inspector whose job it was to persuade high-ranking officers to remain in the force announced that he was leaving Hong Kong before 1997.

Part Two of this book fills out the story of Hong Kong's future, and that of China. The predictions are not based on whim or caprice. They are based on a rigorous, analytical model of group politics with a proven record of accurate, real-time forecasts.

Part Two

Forecasting the Future

❀ 5 ❀

China after Deng

Part I reviewed the conditions that bring us to midnight, 30 June 1997. What happens next? China has made solemn promises. For the next fifty years, Hong Kong is supposed to remain much as it has been. But, as we have seen, words can mean different things to different people. The Chinese government has shown that it interprets its promises in ways that are not consistent with common law and ordinary language. The written word is no guarantee of what the leaders in Beijing will actually do with or to Hong Kong. The remainder of this book concerns predictions, as accurate as possible and more accurate than most believe possible, about the future of Hong Kong.

So many people are writing about Hong Kong's future that you are right to ask why you should pay attention to what we say. What advantage do we have over pundits or experts who offer their thoughts about the years to come? This question deserves a careful answer before you commit another moment to our point of view.

Experts know the history, culture, and facts of life in China and in Hong Kong. Although we are well informed about these important matters, most experts know more facts than we do. But we know more about how policy choices are made than they do. Developments in Hong Kong depend on policy decisions made by leaders in China. Those leaders compete to control policies and to gain political advantages. We are in the unique position of having a well-tested model of just such policy decision making. Facts without a means to interpret them are not especially helpful. Because we have such means, we think you will find our analysis to be very informative. You will understand why events are likely to unfold as we predict and you will be better prepared for the future than if you just listen to experts.

Method of Analysis

To help gain confidence in our approach to policy choices, we digress to introduce you to our method of analysis. We introduced a method for analyzing politics in our 1985 book, *Forecasting Political Events: The Future of Hong Kong*. The predictions in that book have proven to be very accurate. Still, the approach described there has been greatly improved since then. Today we have a dynamic model that predicts how people's policy wishes change and how those wishes influence decisions. The U.S. government and private businesses use this method to predict and influence future policy decisions. In fact, the American Central Intelligence Agency (CIA) has authenticated that this method is accurate more than 90 percent of the time and is much more precise than any other method of studying politics that they know about. We are confident that they know about every sensible approach to policy analysis that has ever been proposed. So, their "seal of approval" is quite reassuring. Also, some of us have published articles that contain dozens of political predictions. The public record bears out the claim of accuracy. You can check it for yourself. Appendix B at the end of this book concludes with a list of published predictions.

Policymaking involves interests competing to influence choices. Political leaders, military officials, bureaucrats, businessmen, foreign governments, ethnic groups, other special interests, and ordinary people are among those who want to shape policy. These groups differ in the intensity and influence that they bring to decisions. They also differ in what they want.

Influence depends on control over resources. Political influence is used to alter the policy wishes of other groups. The object of each stakeholder is to build a strong coalition in favor of the choice he or she and his or her backers desire. Building such a coalition can involve some problems. First, people may disagree about what would be the best decision. If these disagreements exist, it can be hard to find supporters. Second, some competitors are better at shaping decisions than are others. This is true because they control the right resources or because they muster more supporters. Third, everyone compares the costs and benefits of getting what they want and of being seen as a deal maker. Politics is the art of the practical, but not everyone involved in politics is inclined to be practical. Some people believe so deeply in the policy they favor that they are not willing to compromise. They care only about getting what they want. We call getting what you want *policy satisfaction*. Others care so much about being deal makers that they will support any decision they think can win. These people value being part of the winning side as more important than what they actually win. We call the desire to be part of the winning side regardless of the outcome *political satisfaction.* Most people fall in between these extremes. They are willing to make concessions to help forge a deal, but they are not willing to give up everything they believe in. Political bargaining depends on how willing people are to give up the policy they most prefer in order to make a deal. The essence of politics is embodied in the willingness of competitors to trade between policy satisfaction and political satisfaction.

Politics involves cooperation and competition. Groups propose policy compromises or try to coerce opponents into doing what they want. These groups are often centered on well-known or powerful individuals. For instance, throughout our analysis we talk about Li Peng, Jiang Zemin, Qian Qichen, and others as stakeholders. We do not mean to single these individuals out as if by themselves they carry great weight. Although they might, when we refer to individual names as stakeholders we really refer to the bloc of support led by and represented by the individual whose name is given to the group. For stakeholders that lack a single well-known leader, such as the People's Liberation Army (PLA), Western regional cadres, or Hong Kong business interests, we simply name the generic group. This holds true throughout our study and implies that generalizations about, for instance, Li Peng are generalizations about him and his backers. The generalizations should hold true for his backers even if he personally were absent from the scene.

When stakeholders decide on a course of action, they evaluate an elaborate array of choices. Among these is the option to do nothing. If they think their efforts at changing existing circumstances will fail, they live with the current policy or status quo. The process is like a very complicated card game. The decision to live with the current policy is much like "folding" in the game of poker when you have been dealt a particularly poor hand.

In politics it is as if each player is dealt a hand. The quality of the hand depends on the influence, attentiveness, and policy objective of each player. Stronger players (or those with strong backing from others) draw better cards than weaker players. Some players pay closer attention to their cards than do others. This influences their perception of the situation. Based on their influence, attentiveness, and policy objectives, each decision maker forms perceptions about each rival's hand. With that information, each player decides on a strategy of policy proposals to make to some or all of the other players. The content of each proposal is a specific suggestion about a policy that a stakeholder is willing to support or that a stakeholder is seeking support for. The proposed policy need not be the same as what the proposer currently supports.

After all the players submit their secret proposals to one another, each reviews the hand—the proposals—that it holds. Some proposals are better for the recipient than others. Indeed, some proposals turn out to be frivolous. The proposer cannot enforce his bid. Other proposals seem sensible but fall by the wayside because a superior offer was made by a different stakeholder. Each player would like to choose the best offer made to it, and each proposer enforces its bids to the extent that it can. Each actor selects the best offer it receives or the least bad one.

At the end of a round of proposal making, players learn new information. By monitoring responses to their proposals, players learn how much leverage they can exert on other decision makers. If a proposal is accepted, then a player learns that it made the best offer to the recipient of the accepted bid. If a proposal is rejected, the decision maker learns that it could not enforce what it wanted.

When the players finish sorting out their choices, each shifts to the position contained in the proposal it accepted. Of course, when a decision maker agrees to a compromise with someone else, he hopes that the other player will also live up to his end of the bargain. Alas, politics involves promises that are not binding. Proposals are enforced if a decision maker has the strength or support to make sure that others do what they promised to do. Decision makers are free to renege on a proposed deal as long as they can enforce some other agreement or as long as someone else forces an agreement on them.

Policy Satisfaction vs. Political Satisfaction

To predict what proposals are made, which deals are accepted, and how decisions are really made, our model focuses on tradeoffs between policy satisfaction and political satisfaction. We assume that everyone cares about both, but to different degrees. Remember, policy satisfaction involves getting a decision that is consistent with the stakeholder's policy preference. Political satisfaction involves making deals and being part of the winning team. Policy satisfaction often comes at the expense of political satisfaction, and political satisfaction generally involves giving up some policy satisfaction. We model the tradeoff between these two kinds of satisfaction by using what economists call indifference curves. In doing so, we see which proposed deals will be viewed as frivolous and which will be taken seriously. We can also see which compromises on policy will stick and which will not.

Leaders pursue the highest benefits at the lowest cost. Certainly they do not make choices that are expected to leave them worse off than the status quo. In evaluating proposals, decision makers consider how much policy satisfaction and how much political satisfaction each provides. Ideally, any decision maker would like to have infinite policy satisfaction and infinite political satisfaction, but realistically it is likely that some tradeoff has to be made between the two. The problem is to figure out how much of one each stakeholder will sacrifice in exchange for more of the other. We briefly summarize that decision process by sketching the basic intuition behind our analytic approach. Of course, the actual analysis is more complicated and involves a considerable amount of mathematical manipulation (see appendix B).

Let us consider Saddam Hussein's decision making in the days and weeks leading up to the second Gulf War, the one against the United States and its allies. Certainly he was aware that there were many who had an interest either in his getting out of or his staying in Kuwait. Some interested parties were the president of the United States, the prime minister of England, the president of Egypt, the secretary general of the United Nations, the emir of Kuwait, other members of the al Sabah family, Kurdish leaders in Iraq, the Revolutionary Guards, the Tankriti clan in Iraq, and many others.

Each stakeholder can be described as having three important characteristics: a pool of resources, including military might and economic leverage, that could influence the outcome; a level of interest in or salience for the problem; and a preference regarding the best resolution of the dispute. By examining the policy preferences of each stakeholder, Saddam Hussein could evaluate who agreed with his policy, who leaned his way, who favored his opponents, and who was opposed to the outcome he desired. This information would have helped Saddam Hussein evaluate who his supporters and who his adversaries would be in the event of a war or a negotiation. But knowing who was with him and who was against him alone could not determine his course of action. He had also to know how much their support or opposition was worth.

The resources that the stakeholders possess represent the upper boundary of what they could contribute to an effort to carry the day by Saddam Hussein or his adversaries. Resources alone, however, tell a limited story. Saddam Hussein must also have been concerned about the willingness of his allies to make their resources available to him, just as he must have worried about how amenable his enemy's allies were to making resources available to them. That willingness would be influenced by the salience each stakeholder attached to the issue and by the degree to which each stakeholder's policy preference tilted toward Hussein's goals or, say, George Bush's policy objectives. Even stakeholders with tremendous resources might prove to be inconsequential if they did not care enough about the issue or if they were just as happy to see Iraq's objectives prevail as America's objectives.

King Hussein of Jordan, for instance, favored Saddam Hussein's policy. The prime minister of Japan favored the American position. Neither, however, had a great impact on the war's outcome. The Japanese simply did not view the dispute as of sufficient importance to commit more than money—and then relatively little and late—to the effort. King Hussein cared more, but he had too few resources to give. He helped Iraq with words and by opening his border so that the Iraqis could smuggle some goods past the international embargo. Neither Japan nor Jordan was a powerful influence on the outcome. One is a tiny country with little possibility of exerting great influence and the other is the second-largest economy in the world, but with little interest in using its leverage.

Like every other decision maker involved in the months leading up to the Gulf War, Saddam Hussein had to contemplate how resources, salience, and preferences would shape the behavior of all other stakeholders. In doing so, he had to calculate which stakeholders would be responsive to compromises he might propose and which would not. For instance, on the eve of the bombing of Baghdad, the Russians responded to exchanges with the Iraqis by proposing a multilateral conference at which to reach a compromise settlement. Apparently they were not so committed to the American/UN point of view that they could not be influenced by the Iraqis. The Americans, in choosing their own response to the Russian proposal, had to calculate how, for instance, the French and their other allies would respond. In fact, to make that calculation they used an earlier version of the very model used in this book. The Americans apparently concluded that their coalition of allies would hold; they rejected the call for a negotiation and insisted on Iraq's unconditional withdrawal from Kuwait. Hussein had proposed a compromise and the American/UN side rejected it. They preferred to coerce him into submission.

In our model, information about resources, salience, and policy preferences are used to calculate the perceived relationship between each stakeholder and every other stakeholder. The source of that information is discussed below. We estimate what proposal, if any, is best to make to each other participant in the decision process. Sometimes it is best to live with the status quo and propose nothing. Other times, a compromise can be struck that makes each party to the deal better off. One stakeholder might gain policy satisfaction at the expense of political satisfaction, and another might gain political satisfaction at the expense of policy satisfaction. As long as each perceives a net gain, the deal can be made. Still other times, a stakeholder concludes that it has the ability either on its own or with the help of others to coerce an opponent into accepting its point of view. Sometimes efforts at coercion result in the desired outcome, but other times coercion leads to a fight, like the Gulf War, in which both sides think they are strong enough to win. In the case of the Gulf War, Saddam Hussein proved strong enough to survive a decisive military defeat. America and its allies proved strong enough to force the Iraqis out of Kuwait, but George Bush did not prove to be personally strong enough to keep his job as president of the United States.

In our model, as in real life, we do not assume that people always make the best proposal they can. With hindsight, it certainly does not look as if the Iraqi government followed the best available strategy. Instead, we assume that people can make mistakes, but they do so while trying to be as careful as they can be with the limited information they have at the time choices are made. In that sense, we model decision making in a realistic way, taking into account human frailties, misperception, and shortsightedness, each of which can lead to errors in judgment and to undesired or unanticipated outcomes. We focus on the strategic choices stakeholders make before they know how things will turn out. We assume that each stakeholder makes what it believes is the best choice given what it knows at the time a proposal or action must be taken. Hindsight cannot be allowed to color our analytic judgments if predictions and explanations about future decisions are to be accurate.

We present in more detail now the essential elements that go into estimating how decisions are made in politics. The next few pages may contain more material than you want or require. You should feel free to skip them by jumping ahead these few pages. The next section is not essential to understanding the rest of this book. If, however, you read this section and find it intriguing, you might then want to look at the technical appendix (B), which contains more detail on how we make the calculations from which our analysis is derived. That appendix also includes references to still more precise accounts for the truly curious reader. Whether you read the next section or not, we do want you to keep in mind that none of the analysis that follows is based on our personal opinions or personal preferences. The analysis is the product of applying an explicit, logical framework to basic information about stakeholders interested in the future of China and Hong Kong.

In figure 5.1 we represent the possible tradeoff between policy satisfaction and political satisfaction on a graph. The horizontal axis represents how much political satisfaction a choice provides, and the vertical axis represents how much policy satisfaction it gives. For some readers labeling the horizontal axis "income" and the vertical axis "leisure time" may make this discussion easier to grasp. Imagine that point X repre-

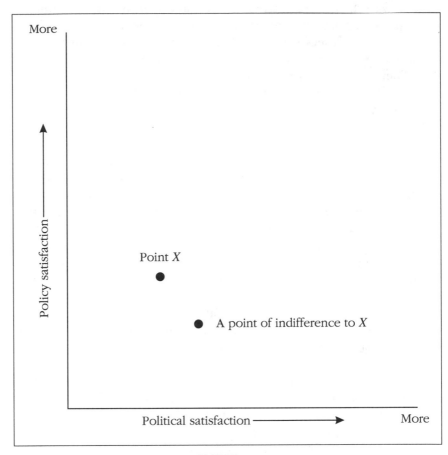

FIGURE 5.1
THE TRADEOFF BETWEEN POLICY SATISFACTION
AND POLITICAL SATISFACTION

sents a choice that is expected to give a certain amount of policy satisfaction (leisure time) and a certain amount of political satisfaction (income). Now imagine that there is another choice with less policy satisfaction (leisure time) than offered by choice X, but with just enough extra political satisfaction (income) so as to make the second choice equally appealing to the decision maker. This second choice is at a *point of indifference* relative to the first choice. It is a point that represents an alternative with a different mix of conditions than X, but which is still an acceptable alternative for that decision maker—it is neither better nor worse than X.

If we plot all the points of indifference to point X, we get what is called an *indifference curve*. As the name implies, the decision maker is

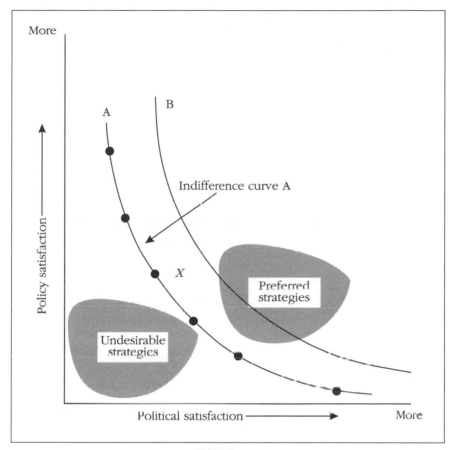

FIGURE 5.2
THE INDIFFERENCE CURVE

equally satisfied with the mix of policy and political benefits (leisure time and income) for any point on the indifference curve. The decision maker prefers deals that yield benefits above the curve to those on the curve, and the leader prefers choices on the curve to points below it. This is true because points above the curve give as much satisfaction on one dimension as a point on the curve and give more satisfaction on the other dimension (points above the curve relative to points on the curve reflect combinations of more leisure time and more income). Points below the curve have the opposite characteristic. They can give equal satisfaction on one dimension but give less satisfaction on the other. Figure 5.2 shows an example of two indifference curves, A and B. B is higher than

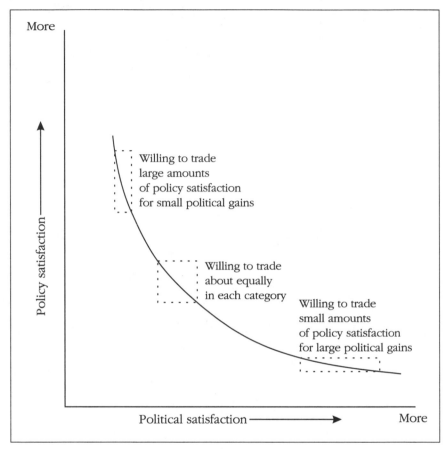

More

Political satisfaction

Willing to trade
large amounts
of policy satisfaction
for small political gains

Willing to trade
about equally
in each category

Willing to trade
small amounts
of policy satisfaction
for large political gains

Political satisfaction ⟶   More

FIGURE 5.3
DIFFERENT VALUES ALONG THE INDIFFERENCE CURVE

A. This means that the decision maker prefers any mix of policy satisfaction and political satisfaction (leisure time and income) on B to any mix on A. If X is the status quo, then all points on curve B improve on the status quo for the decision maker in question.

Every mix of policy satisfaction and political satisfaction (leisure time and income) lies on some indifference curve. As we suggested in describing figure 5.1, points on higher indifference curves are always preferred to points on lower curves. This is made clear in figure 5.2.

The tradeoff that a decision maker is willing to make between policy satisfaction and political satisfaction (leisure time and income) is not the same everywhere on an indifference curve, as you can see in figure

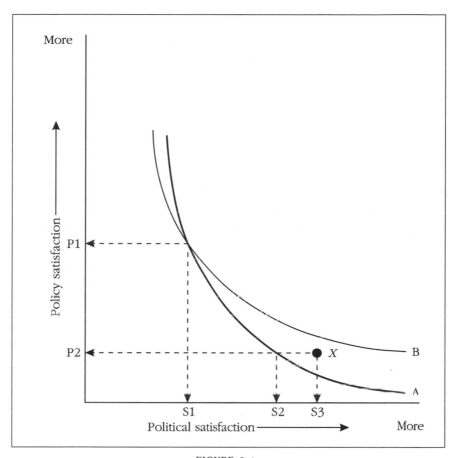

FIGURE 5.4
THE SHAPE OF THE INDIFFERENCE CURVE

5.3. In the middle of the curve, policy outcomes and political outcomes (leisure time and income) or deal making are valued about equally. At the top or bottom, one of the two sources of satisfaction becomes more valuable to the decision maker. This makes sense, for example, because a leader wants to maintain at least some political (income) and at least some policy (leisure time) satisfaction. As the amount of political satisfaction (income) approaches zero, the amount of policy satisfaction (leisure time) that the leader would trade away for political satisfaction (income) increases dramatically.

Different decision makers can have indifference curves with different shapes. The decision maker may care more about one type of satisfaction than the other. For instance, in figure 5.4 we show two decision makers, A and B. A is willing to trade away larger amounts of policy satisfaction (leisure time) for smaller amounts of political satisfaction (income) than is B. A would be just as happy to have policy satisfaction (leisure time) at the level P1 (which is quite high) as to have policy satisfaction (leisure time) at the much lower level P2 provided that political satisfaction (income) would increase from S1 (which is rather low) to S2. Notice that the drop from P1 to P2 is larger than the increase from S1 to S2. This suggests that political benefits (income) are more important to this decision maker than is the policy satisfaction (leisure time) he or she derives. That is why this leader would be willing to make a large policy (leisure time) concession in order to gain a relatively small increase in political (income) benefits.

Other leaders, like B, might have indifference curves with quite different shapes, suggesting different rates at which political and policy (income and leisure time) satisfaction can be exchanged. For instance, B cares more about policy (leisure time) satisfaction than does A. B would not accept a mix of political and policy (income and leisure time) satisfaction such as is suggested at point X on figure 5.4. A, however, would be very pleased to receive the benefits implied by point X. Point X is below B's indifference curve, but it is above A's.

Notice that for leader A, point X provides just as much policy (leisure time) satisfaction as does the choice consistent with political (income) benefits at point S2. X, however, gives the leader extra political (income) satisfaction (S3 is bigger than S2). Consequently, A is better off with X than with the satisfaction available from the combination of S2 and P2. B is not.

The shape of the indifference curve, then, tells us the range in which a large concession in terms of policy (leisure time) satisfaction is worth a small improvement in political (income) benefits for each decision maker. The rate at which tradeoffs are made influences the ease with which deals can be struck with different decision makers. One of the unique features of our approach is that we have developed ways to estimate the shape of each decision maker's indifference curve for each issue. And we can also estimate where the status quo falls on each indifference curve. With this information we estimate what deals each decision maker will propose and what deals each stakeholder will accept.

The perspective we have just outlined is explained more fully in other places. A complete explanation involves a great deal of mathematical exposition to translate our simple ideas about how people choose into a precise model of what goes on in people's heads. Bruce Bueno de Mesquita and Frans Stokman's *European Community Decision Making* provides a technical explanation for those who want to wade through it. The brief outline here should be enough to give you the flavor of our logic.

When we examine the likelihood of Chinese regionalization we will walk you through the interpretation of Jiang Zemin's indifference curve and that of Li Peng as estimated using our method. We explain what these and other leaders' indifference curves imply about policy flexibility on questions of regional or central domination of the government. We also introduce simpler graphs that summarize a great deal of information based on our analysis. Once that is done, we no longer show you the indifference curves we have estimated. Instead, we focus on broader indicators from our model that inform us about likely developments and we explain the unfolding story of China's and Hong Kong's future. In doing so, we ask you to bear in mind that our arguments are based on careful logic and analysis, even though we do not burden you with the analytic details at every point along the way.

Practical Applications

Before turning to the analysis of China after Deng and then, in chapter 6, to the anticipated future for Hong Kong, a brief discussion of how we turn our analytic ideas into practical application is in order. Doing so, of course, requires that we obtain data on the relevant variables, namely, who the stakeholders are, what resources they can potentially bring to bear on a decision, what outcome each desires, and how salient a given issue is to a decision maker during the time that a choice must be made. The data are derived through intensive interviews with experts on the issues that concern us. These experts do not necessarily agree with the conclusions we have derived. Indeed, one valuable feature of the model we are using is that it has proven in thousands of applications to lead to quite accurate predictions that often differ from those made by the very experts whose data inform our investigation.

Since we are using an abstract model fed with data collected from experts on China and Hong Kong, we must be concerned about any biases. We sought information on who will try to influence policies that affect Hong Kong. We asked each expert we consulted to provide quantitative estimates of the policy objectives, the potential influence, and the importance attached to different issues for each group or individual who wants to influence China's or Hong Kong's future. The backgrounds of the experts were quite varied. One is a long-time expatriate resident, active in journalism, business, and government service. Another is a very prominent journalist for a major Chinese newspaper. Still another is a prominent British businessman with a strong pro-Chinese outlook. Several distinguished academic specialists were also consulted, some of them expatriates and others Chinese. Some academics in China proper were also consulted. Additionally, we sought information from local politicians in Hong Kong. Because they all were promised anonymity, we are unable to thank them publicly for the great assistance they provided. Still, it is important to recognize that we did not ask any of the experts what they think will happen in China or Hong Kong. They only provided basic information that a true expert would know. That basic information can be obtained simply by writing to any one of the authors for it.

We selected specialists whose personal political views cover the range. Some were very pro-Chinese; others were quite opposed to the People's Republic. Most were Chinese, but some were not. The experts were not selected for their political leanings but for the information they possessed. In each case we sought only the basic information outlined above. The experts were each asked to provide data on a common set of issues. Despite their personal differences in outlook, *all of the analyses produced essentially the same story.* We did not combine the data from different experts. Instead, we analyzed each set separately, using the computer-based model we have just discussed. Because of the consistency in the results, we are confident that whatever biases our specialists brought to the process were filtered out by our information-gathering techniques and by the logic of our model. The high level of consistency gives us great confidence that the model results are right, whatever the personal judgments of the people who provided information. Indeed, as noted earlier, other uses of this model have revealed that it often yields predictions that are different from the expectations of those experts who provided information. As a declassified CIA study states about this model, whenever its predictions disagreed with the expectations of the intelligence community or the experts who provided data, the model proved right. The interested reader can find a discussion of this point in an article by Stanley Feder in *Studies in Intelligence* for 1987. With this in mind, we turn to the investigation of China's and Hong Kong's future.

Modern China

Visitors to China are struck by the construction going on in every corner of the land. New buildings, new offices, and new shops rise one after the other. The signs of economic growth excite the imagination. The world's most populous nation may soon become its largest market, largest producer, largest consumer, and largest military power. China obviously profits from its economic expansion and from using Hong Kong as an outlet for its goods. Hong Kong is a dynamic source of capital for China and a channel for the People's Liberation Army (PLA), the Communist Party, and others who feel the urge to invest. Average incomes have risen more than 100 percent since 1978. Imports and exports have increased by an astonishing twentyfold. During the 1980s, China's exports to Hong Kong increased tenfold, with a 1,500 percent increase in imports coming from Hong Kong. Certainly if current trends continue, China will emerge in the next few decades as one of the world's great economic engines promoting prosperity among its fifth of the world's population.

Many find it difficult to imagine Chinese leaders following policies that undermine the promise of prosperity. And yet it will be most difficult for them to do otherwise. However committed China may be to economic expansion and to maintaining Hong Kong's affluence, uncertainty about China's political and social future will stymie growth.

Those who are most optimistic say that the clock can never be turned back. They think that China is unalterably committed to economic policies that will lead to prosperity. The optimists are sure that economic objectives dominate political concerns. How quickly they forget the ease with which the Chinese government risked its economic goals in 1989 when its tanks crushed student dissenters. Whenever political ambition or ideological fervor has clashed with the marketplace, politics has won.

The communist dynasty of the past four decades, like the Ch'in, the T'ang, the Yüan, the Ming, and so many others in the long history of the Chinese people, is coming to an end. The next few years will witness no ordinary succession of political power. Instead, China as we know it is likely to unravel. Central authority will be diminished and regional hegemony will rise. Every governmental institution will undergo a major transformation as political, social, economic, and military control slip away from the Communist Party and into the hands of entrepreneurs. These new leaders will be more concerned with their income than with their political control.

At first blush, the story of China's future might inspire optimism. Chinese people are increasingly free to pursue business opportunities. Today, the only place in the world where the average Chinese person is poor is in China. Tomorrow, perhaps that will no longer be true. But getting to tomorrow may cost China its prospects for making the twenty-first century China's century. Dynastic transitions rarely happen peacefully. Civil war, institutional change, and the rise of new, inexperienced leaders are not a recipe for investor confidence. China's transition to an entrepreneurial society may set it back decades in its quest to become the world's largest marketplace. The picture over the next few decades may be gloomy indeed; gloomy for Hong Kong, gloomy for the struggling poor of China, and gloomy for those who aspire to see the emergence of Chinese hegemony.

What are the pieces that will determine the pattern over the coming decades? Why is China expected to undergo a dynastic-like transition, accompanied by internal conflict that may choke economic expansion and diminish Hong Kong's stature in the world of emerging markets? These are the questions we try to answer here, based not on crystal-ball gazing, but on a careful assessment of what is implied in our analysis by widely accepted facts about today's China.

During the past two decades, the Communist Party has endorsed sweeping economic reforms. The partial liberation of business has resulted in double-digit growth rates. Although most Chinese remain desperately poor, today there are millionaires throughout China, and there is the prospect of many more in the years to come. But economic reform has always been cut short when it implies fundamental political change. Prime Minister Li Peng, the darling of the conservatives, is already pushing to reintroduce state central planning. For the communists, after all, the entry of capitalism into China was to spur the realization of the communist state and not to transform it into a capitalist one. Thus it is that property rights remain elusive. The government still owns much of the economy. Contracts for new enterprises are not private agreements between investors; they are products of opaque rules designed to foster governmental control and corruption. More often than not, big deals depend on "greasing the wheel" of government rather than on the Confucian merit system.

Immediately following the communist takeover in 1949, the Shanghai stock market continued to function. Trading went on until the government concluded that it was too easy to lose money speculating on stocks. The market was shut down. In 1987 the Chinese leadership expressed a similar view. When the stock market took a nose dive, the notion was expressed that competition was good, but too much competition was destructive. The government leaders apparently believed that buying low and selling high was not only the right thing to do; it was the only thing to do. Today, fifty years after the revolution, many in the West naively believe that such a simplistic view of economic risk taking has no place in modern China. Yet the Chinese are widely speculated to have repeatedly manipulated the Hong Kong stock market and to have suspended trading on several of their markets just because they did not like the situation at the moment.

The most visible confrontation to date between economic progress and political change occurred in May and June 1989. With wealth comes a natural demand to have a greater say in how the wealth is used. Demands for more freedom are an inevitable by-product of economic success. Students gathered at Tiananmen Square to ask for modest political change. They did not call for the end to communist rule. They did not call for the demise of the Communist Party. They asked for reforms that, if granted, would have left the Chinese, by Western standards, a people still dominated by their government. They sought open investigations of corruption, favoritism, and nepotism by the government. The protestors sought accountability from their leaders.

In only a short time, the student protests expanded to become a broad-based movement for democracy in China. For a few brief weeks, the world watched the blooming of the Beijing Spring, confident that the Chinese authorities would not place their newfound economic success at risk. The *Hong Kong Standard,* for instance, wrote on 8 May 1989 of "Signs of Hope from Beijing," contending that "a crackdown on these students would have frightened off the investors China needs badly.... China's leaders know their country is plugged into the global mainstream and that they must therefore take cognisance of the effects of their actions on the rest of the world.... For the very first time the pragmatists have openly shown that they are prepared to defy the older leaders and to carry out their own rational, moderate decisions."

Tragically, less than one month later, this optimistic view proved dead wrong. Just as quickly as the flower of democracy bloomed, so too did it wilt before the guns and tanks of China's 27th Army. Amid the rubble left behind from the weekend of 4 June lay hundreds, perhaps thousands, of dead protesters. Zhao Ziyang, one-time leader of the Chinese Communist Party—one of the pragmatists believed to have taken charge—was in disrepute. Li Peng and Deng Xiaoping reasserted their control over China's political life.

The crackdown at Tiananmen Square by the army carried with it grave risks that world markets would close to Chinese goods. Economic sanctions were the likely weapon of choice by the Western powers. Yet the leadership did not hesitate for long. Force was used against demonstrators who had done nothing violent and who had demanded nothing extraordinary by Western standards. Zhao Ziyang, the one high-ranking leader to express sympathy for the students, was cast aside. He became a nonperson in the party hierarchy. Reform met its limits when the privileges of the elite were put at risk.

The story of Tiananmen Square is an indicator of what is likely to come. Today the same issues of corruption, favoritism, and nepotism dominate debate in China. Contending forces use these issues to imprison political foes. Competition rages over who is to be, in the long run, Deng Xiaoping's successor. In the process, the competition is shifting from a dispute within the party to a dispute across almost every segment of life in China.

The core competition within China that would reflect a normal succession crisis involves such well-known figures as Li Peng (prime minister) and Jiang Zemin (president), and perhaps lesser known leaders such as Li Ruihuan (politburo member and chairman, Consultative Conference) and Zhu Rongji (vice premier). Political competition is no longer limited to these officials, nor are their key constituents restricted any more to party cadres. Today succession in China must reflect a balance between central party officials and regional elites, especially business interests in the coastal and southern provinces. Before, succession was a matter to be determined in Beijing. Now, the dynastic transition may be determined in Beijing, but it may alternatively be determined in Fujian, Canton, and Shanghai.

The issue of greatest concern today is where authority will lie in China. Is China's immediate future tied to a highly centralized state like that developed by Mao Zedong or to a weak confederacy of regional interests similar to the government in America under the Articles of Confederation? A decentralized confederacy is a common form of government for new states with regional differences. The United States started with just such arrangements. So too have the states of the former Soviet Union. Confederacy did not last more than a decade in the United States and may not last much longer in Russia and the associated republics. In Switzerland a weak central government, dominated by referendum voting in the cantons, has persisted for about a century and a half. How long a weak center can last in China is unknown, but it is clear to us that a strong center cannot persist for more than a few years. China's immediate future is as a decentralized, highly federalized union. Federalism will revolve around economic, ethnic, and political interests.

Why is this so? The goals of regional and central authorities are fragmented. As figure 5.5 shows, a chasm separates the current perspective of the regional and centrist interests. Nevertheless, we believe that in time most of the centrists—the currently dominant leaders in China—will be forced to accept a new reality. In that new reality most current leaders will have to grant provincial authorities greater influence over political life.

In figure 5.5 we have plotted the effects of all of the variables that inform our analysis. On the horizontal axis we show policy preferences regarding centralism or regionalism as the primary source of political authority in China. Low values reflect a desire to keep China highly centralized, while high values reflect a preference for decentralization with

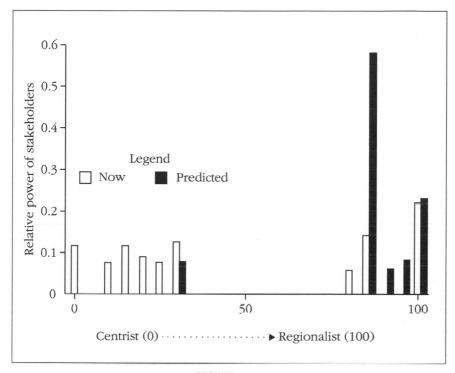

FIGURE 5.5
REGIONALIST-CENTRIST COMPETITION IN CHINA

authority passing to regional leaders. The vertical axis, labeled "Relative power of stakeholders," shows the percentage of political influence clustered at each policy position staked out as the desired outcome by one or more decision makers. Political influence is defined as the product of the resources each stakeholder can exert on an issue and the salience or importance each stakeholder attaches to the issue. So, if a stakeholder has control over 20 percent of relevant resources, but attaches only 10 percent importance to the issue, then that stakeholder contributes 10 percent of its 20 percent of resources, or a total of 2 percent. That measure of influence is shown for the present as unshaded bars. The predicted future distribution of influence after bargaining on this issue is shown as dark bars. What is especially noteworthy in figure 5.5 is that the unshaded bars are fairly evenly distributed across policy preferences, with no great peaks, but without any support in the center of the issue range. The dark bars, by contrast, are more closely clustered at the high end of the scale that reflects movement toward regional control. And there is one great peak of support among the dark bars for a system in which a modest role is still reserved for the center. That is the implication of the tall dark bar at position 80 on the issue scale—reflecting a considerable devolution of power to the regions.

Not all central leaders are expected to give in to pressure from provincial entrepreneurs. Indeed, we anticipate that the conflict over regional influence is likely to start as a struggle between Li Peng and Jiang Zemin for control over the party. Each feels a need to distinguish himself from the pack of would-be new leaders in China. Jiang Zemin will try to curry favor with the monied interests in the provinces. He believes this is his best path to political control. For Li Peng, the strategy is to try and work within the party framework. He will try to build support among the hard-line party ideologues and the military. Jiang Zemin's approach leads him quickly to accept the perspective of the provincial authorities. Li Peng, by contrast, distinguishes himself from the pack by standing firmly and squarely behind the status quo. This will leave him isolated and defeated.

The conclusions about Jiang Zemin and Li Peng are easily discerned from our estimation of indifference curves. Figure 5.6 shows our approximation of the shape of the indifference curves for these two leaders on the issue of regionalization. The curves are somewhat bumpy, reflecting the fact that our estimation method is not perfect. Still, it is quite evident that our analysis shows that Jiang Zemin is willing to give up much of what he truly wishes on the policy dimension for political gains. He is willing to sacrifice the center's authority in exchange for his political advancement, while Li Peng is not. If they both start out fully satisfied with the status quo of central authority, the figure shows us that Li Peng would give up about 60 percent (1.00 −.40) of his policy satisfaction only if he gained an almost equal amount of political benefits (from 0 to about .33). An equal sacrifice in policy preference from Jiang Zemin can be purchased more cheaply. He would give up 60 percent of his satisfaction with the status quo, supporting much more regional authority instead, in exchange for just a 10 percent improvement in his political well-being. This means that he is a more attractive person for provincial authorities to bargain with than is Li Peng. Therefore, we predict that provincial leaders will succeed in persuading Jiang Zemin to back more regionalization of China while failing to persuade Li Peng. Of course, similar comparisons can be made across all of the stakeholders included in our analysis.

Competition between the central and provincial authorities is expected to involve intense conflict. Because the anticipated changes are fundamental, there is little room for the normal give-and-take of routine

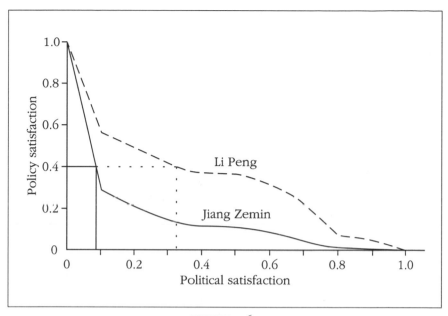

FIGURE 5.6
REGIONALIZATION OF CHINA.
INDIFFERENCE CURVES: JIANG ZEMIN, LI PENG

politics. The unusual nature of the situation is evident in figure 5.5, displayed on page 87. In particular, notice that the distribution of power and interests starts out being polarized. There is a huge gulf of emptiness in the center of the political spectrum. No one favors a genuine compromise that would involve real power sharing between the center and the provinces. Instead, the Old Guard wants to keep things pretty much as is, and the regional-entrepreneurs want a radical shift in authority to them. To give a sense of how unusual this polarization is, we provide figures 5.7 and 5.8 (p. 90). In these figures we contrast the general structure of politics in China with structures of politics in more typical, stable political settings such as are found in Britain, France, Japan, and the United States. In figure 5.7 we see two blocs pulling in opposite directions, with few groups in the middle able to moderate decisions. In these circumstances, policy can rapidly shift as one or another side gains a short-run advantage. In figure 5.8, policies are more stable, as there is a consensus of powerful groups regarding policy, and those supporting the consensus are never far from the actual policy adopted.

Polarized interests such as characterize contemporary China often

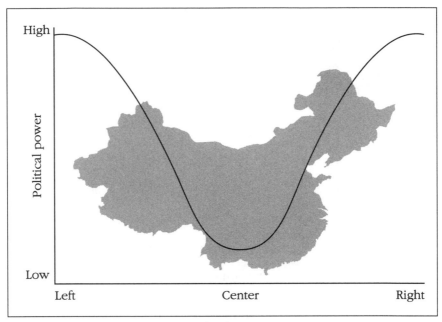

FIGURE 5.7
POLITICAL POLARIZATION IN CHINA

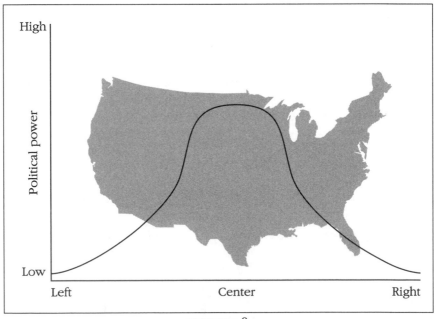

FIGURE 5.8
POLITICAL POLARIZATION IN THE UNITED STATES

lead to system-wrenching disputes over the fundamental political "rules of the game." China is no exception.

Political competition takes on only *five patterns*. Naturally, allies usually can (1) *agree* with one another about a policy choice, providing support for each other's objectives. Sometimes, however, even allies do not fully agree. In such cases, they look for ways (2) to *compromise,* producing normal, incremental political change. But different interests sometimes fear trying to compromise because they believe such efforts will backfire, leaving them worse off. In such cases, (3) *stalemate* follows. The status quo prevails even if no one is happy with it. Other times, one set of interests is sufficiently powerful that it need not compromise and need not fear giving up the status quo. Powerful political actors may simply (4) *coerce* others into doing their bidding. Whenever a political power can coerce others into submission, it will do so. After all, the object of politics is to win the competition for control over office, policy, and resources. Finally, sometimes each of two or more groups may think it can compel the others to submit to its will. Decision makers who share such a view are likely to come into (5) *conflict* with one another. Who will win the contest of wills cannot be known at the outset. If it were known, one decision maker would coerce the other into submission, or the weaker party would concede right away. Instead, a war of sorts wages until one or the other gives in.

Routine politics is typified by lots of compromising and occasional stalemates between competitors. Conflict and coercion are not the stuff of daily politics. They are the stuff of civil war, revolution, and fundamental political change. We find China's internal politics, especially over questions related to the balance of power between regional and central interests, to be the stuff of civil war and fundamental institutional upheaval. Consider the pie chart in figure 5.9 (p. 92).

It shows the current relationship between more than a dozen key interest groups in China who are trying to influence the roles of the center and provinces. The calculation of the mix of political relationships shown in the figure is the result of our analysis. By examining the indifference curves and estimates of the perceptions of each stakeholder vis-à-vis each other, we are able to distinguish situations that imply agreement, compromise, stalemate, coercion, and conflict. For instance, if two decision makers misjudge each other's inclinations to trade policy satisfaction and political satisfaction, each might make a proposal to the other that the proposer views as perfectly sensible. Yet each proposal might be rejected by its recipient because it does not give enough on one dimension to compensate for sacrifices asked for on the other dimension. Such a situation might trigger a conflict, with each decision maker think-

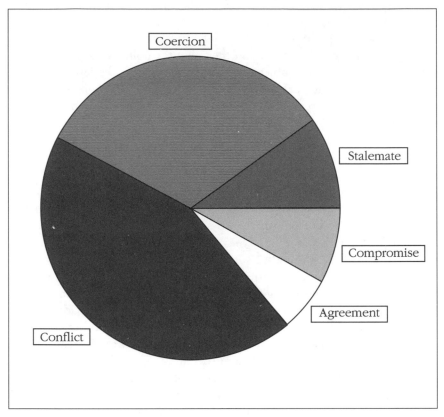

FIGURE 5.9
REGIONALISM OR CENTRISM IN CHINA?
A DYNASTIC TRANSITION

ing the other is trying to take advantage of it. Figure 5.9 summarizes our calculations about how the stakeholders will relate to one another.

Appendix B explains the computer-generated printout that our model produces. There we provide a sample analysis of PLA relationships on a specific issue. One of the model's outputs examines the pairwise relationship between, in this case, the PLA and each other group. Those summaries depict the relationships estimated by our model from three perspectives: the PLA's view of its relationship with everyone else, everyone else's view of their relationships with the PLA, and our model-based evaluation of how those perceived relationships translate into actual interactions. Of course, there is a comparable analysis for each stakeholder. Figures such as the pie chart in figure 5.9 assess the overall political climate on the issue in question by depicting the proportion of relationships that satisfy the logical conditions for conflict (each side thinks it can force the other side to accept its point of view); coercion (one side believes it can force the other to accept its point of view, and the other concurs); stalemate (neither side thinks it can get the other to agree to its proposals); compromise (one side thinks it can persuade the other to shift its position somewhat in the direction desired by the first group, and the second group concurs); and agreement (both sides share the same policy objective).

The pie chart indicates that few agreements or compromises are likely between regional and central authorities. Coercion and conflict are the main expected forms of political exchange. The pie chart and the analysis on which it is based provide little reason to be optimistic about China's transition to a new form of government. In the end the new government may boost freedom and prosperity. That stage will be reached, however, only after a period of high risk of violence and turmoil.

The balkanization of real political control raises more questions than it answers. If China's provincial authorities rise in influence, what will this mean for the future role of the PLA? What will be the consequence of regionalism for the resolution of the central succession crisis in Beijing? How will all these factors influence commitments to economic reform?

THE MILITARY

The future of the military is crucial to the unfolding prospects for China. China's military is as much an arm of the Communist Party as it is an arm of the state. It protects the party's interests, and, in exchange, its members enjoy great privileges. Because the central party leaders need the PLA's support, they promote and protect the army's interests. Still, tension exists because some military leaders derive their main benefits from their provincial ties. The PLA is possibly the most active sector of the government when it comes to participation in economic growth. Indeed, the *Far Eastern Economic Review* estimates that the PLA actively participates in as many as 20,000 companies, ranging from legitimate businesses to illegal enterprises. The PLA's businesses include hotels, pharmaceutical firms, and bordellos, for instance. Nearly 50 percent of the instances of piracy in the South China Sea—and piracy is not a rare event in that part of the world—are attributed to Chinese naval units.

Navy ships routinely transport goods—some legally obtained, others the fruits of piracy—from Hong Kong to the mainland and back. Huge profits are enjoyed by naval officers for promoting such uses of the vessels under their command. It is estimated that many PLA companies derive as much as 80 percent of their revenues from civilian activities. Most of the truck traffic in China is now thought to involve military vehicles moving goods to market. Again, huge profits are involved. After 1997, the PLA will become a major investor and real estate developer in Hong Kong as it acquires certain pieces of property, owning upward of HK$100 billion in property. Military leaders who participate in regional business ventures do not want to lose their comparative advantage. They do not want the center to wrest business opportunities away from their provincial backers.

The military is torn between its commitments to central authorities and to regional elites. The gravy train enjoyed by the military can persist only as long as China is ruled by corruption instead of law. Some members of the PLA, therefore, have strong interests in protecting the status quo. Others, divorced from the corruption associated with private uses of public equipment, are committed to building a professional military.

The PLA is about to enter a roller-coaster ride. Figures 5.10a and 5.10b show how attitudes toward the military are expected to evolve in the next few years. The lines running across the graph depict the predicted changes in policy positions of key groups in China over the next few years. These predictions, of course, are the product of our analytic model and not our personal judgments or those of the experts who provided data. They reflect the evaluation of all proposals that are predicted by our model to be made and to be accepted or rejected. The shifts in group positions reflect the proposals predicted to be accepted.

The "outcome" line captures the overall central push toward change that reflects the pulls and tugs of all stakeholders, not just those displayed in the figure. That line, showing the predicted future of the PLA, bumps up and down. This signifies great swings between support for a politicized military and a professional military, reflecting the PLA's commitment to political satisfaction ahead of policy satisfaction. Lower values on the vertical scale reflect support for a military that serves the state and not party interests. In addition to predicting that the government will fall more under regional control, we expect that the military will become more professional in a few years. But before it reaches the end of the roller-coaster ride, China will undergo an upheaval. Soon there will be an experiment to make the military more professional. Some central authorities, especially the Old Guard leaders, will view the experiment as a failure. They will steadfastly support a politicized PLA. This is seen in the straight line at the top of the figure. Others, such as Jiang Zemin and Li Peng, will shift in their attitude. Ultimately, the party will lose control over the PLA and it will be professionalized. The end is good for China, but the process of getting there is likely to be costly. We

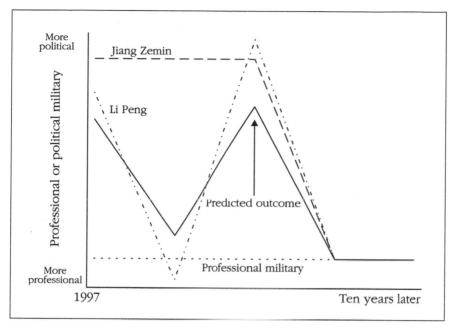

FIGURE 5.IOA

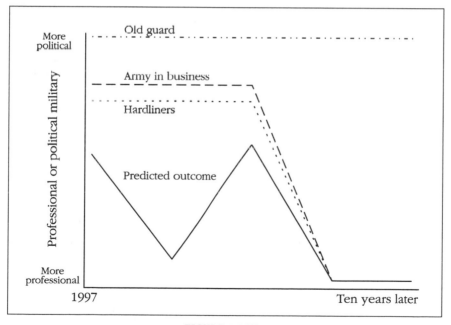

FIGURE 5.IOB
FUTURE ROLE OF THE PLA

predict that the great swings will produce a high level of uncertainty about the future. Such uncertainty cannot help economic growth or political stability over the next few years.

There are several reasons for the anticipated instability in the future of the PLA. On this question, as with regional competition, we find Chinese interests to be polarized. Again, no one occupies a middle ground. This means no one is naturally positioned to take the lead on building a consensus. Also, the future of the PLA is closely tied to the impending long-term succession crisis. Li Peng is eager to gain support from the military. He has stuck his finger in the air to see which way the wind is blowing. At first he takes a tough stand to protect the status quo. But when he notices that many military leaders endorse the idea of a more professional PLA, as reflected in their unwavering position in figure 5.10a, he jumps on that bandwagon. Later, Li reacts to the opposition from important Old Guard leaders who do not support this change. He swings back to his original hard-line position. But this change in attitude does not last long. Seeing the consensus moving in favor of professionalizing the military, Li Peng swings again, ultimately going along with the mainstream.

Li's *flexibility* reflects his fear of losing support among significant powers in Beijing. On this important question, he is eager to protect his political satisfaction even at the expense of the policy he really wants. He fails to understand that power is moving to the provinces. Because of this, his opportunistic shifts in attitude will jeopardize his future political influence and also cost him policy satisfaction.

We believe that Li Peng's star will fizzle after an intense struggle. Jiang, by contrast, also starts with a hard-line position. But he comes to recognize that the future lies away from Beijing. He joins provincial leaders in pushing for a more professional military, sticking by his guns even though that is costly in the mid-term. In the longer run, when the regional interests dominate the center, Jiang is a potential winner because of his perceived commitment to proregional changes. Key among his commitments is his decision to support professionalizing the PLA.

ECONOMIC REFORM

Against the backdrop of political turmoil is the question of how China will fare economically. Our previous results suggest a depressing view and this is borne out here. The evidence and logic of our study make us quite pessimistic. Economic issues will be used by all sides to polarize Chinese politics. They will succeed, as is evident in figure 5.11.

Figure 5.11 reflects a part of China's schizophrenia regarding economic reforms. We look at three general time periods: immediately after

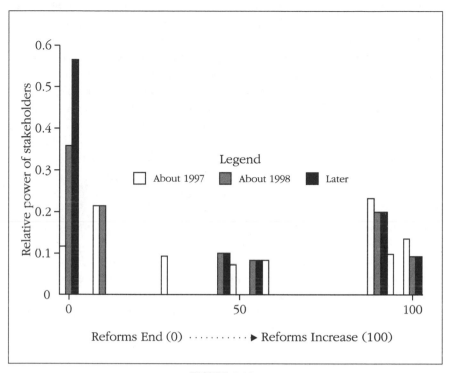

FIGURE 5.11
FUTURE OF ECONOMIC REFORM

Hong Kong reverts to China, perhaps one year later, and further beyond. Several factors are worth noting.

In the early period there is considerable disagreement about economic reform. Some interest groups are very enthusiastic about expanding market conditions in China. Not least among these are the various military factions with ties to the provinces, many of whom want a professionalized PLA or just plain want to keep their business opportunities open in the provinces, and those who are exploiting business opportunities through their ties to the center. But there are also important interests who want to put an end to China's fascination with capitalist markets. Party hard-liners and Li Peng are among them. Jiang Zemin starts off somewhat more moderately. He wants to continue existing efforts, but he is opposed to expanding economic reforms.

Our model shows that economic reform will continue for the time being; however, there is likely to be a sudden and dramatic collapse of support for market reforms. Figure 5.11 shows a big swing of power in the second period. This swing is accentuated in the third period, as is evident from the tall, dark bar. By then, a majority of the powerful interests in China oppose continuing economic reforms. At the same time, the distribution of powerful interests reflects deep divisions in opinion. Many moderates disappear on this issue. In the end those who strongly back economic change, including regional authorities and, ultimately, Jiang Zemin, stand at loggerheads with the antireformists. The military sides with the monied interests against the party. The balance of power on this matter rests with the party officials, but it is a fragile balance. Small changes in leadership or influence over the coming years can easily tilt the balance the other way. But whether the balance lies in favor of economic reform or against it will not matter that much. What will matter is that the country becomes deeply divided and that uncertainty will likely deal a serious blow to growth.

What will this mean for China's general approach to Hong Kong? China has promised to preserve Hong Kong's free-market economy for at least fifty years. But political troubles in China will probably force a reexamination of such promises. Indeed, we believe that Hong Kong will fall victim to the political upheaval between central and regional powers. The slowing of economic progress will not happen without harming Hong Kong.

Hong Kong's Autonomy

In figure 5.12 we compare the relationships among key decision makers now and in a few years regarding Hong Kong's autonomy. With all the political strife expected in the next few years, we want to know whether China can keep its promise to protect Hong Kong's freedom. Given the solemn promises and international agreements signed by China, this should not be a controversial question. But it is. We find that the issue is becoming increasingly conflictual. As time unfolds, China's leaders fail to work out a common understanding of how to deal with Hong Kong. Instead, relations will deteriorate, as shown by the increasing number of conflictual and coercive relationships, as some see China reneging on its promises and others see Hong Kong as a tool in the political struggle between the party and provincial leaders.

Disagreements about Hong Kong's future role will presage a breakdown in China's commitments. We anticipate that Hong Kong's autonomy will be eroded quickly, only to be restored for a period of a year or so. But after the period of restored autonomy, we anticipate a deep retrenchment by China. Hong Kong will be an instrument of political strife

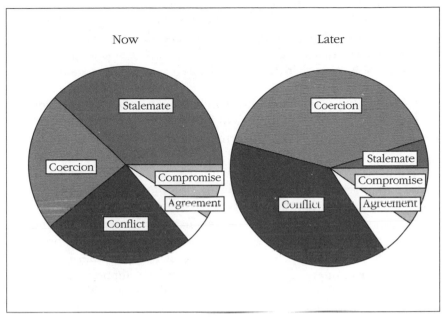

FIGURE 5.12
TURMOIL AND HONG KONG'S AUTONOMY

and control. In such a setting, autonomy for Hong Kong cannot and will not be tolerated. China will pull back from its international promises.

The Old Guard leaders of the party built their careers on economic policy. They will not renege on China's promised autonomy for Hong Kong. It means too much to them. Our study reveals that they are steadfast supporters of the agreements they made on Hong Kong's autonomy. Instead, the business interests in the military, the party ideologues, and many Western regional cadres will jump ship, abandoning the Old Guard and betraying the international promises made by China because it suits their personal interests to do so. They fear economic (and political) competition from an autonomous Hong Kong. Therefore they prefer to keep Hong Kong under the government's thumb. In this way, they protect their access to wealth and markets. Their access depends on corruption rather than competition. Consequently, they cannot flourish for long if Hong Kong is really autonomous.

Hong Kong's autonomy is in grave jeopardy because of the unholy alliance of die-hard communists, greedy military officers, and greedy regional elites. Here, then, we see an odd coalition. On most issues the regional elites and the party ideologues are at opposite ends of the spectrum. On the question of Hong Kong, however, they agree. This bodes particularly ill for Hong Kong's future because this is at once a powerful alliance and one that is difficult to break apart. Greed is a powerful motivator in politics and in life. It will surely play against Hong Kong's future.

We expect that the years ahead will be a period of economic consolidation in China. Few new steps will be taken to expand property rights or normalize business activity. Retrenchment is not likely, but neither is more progress in institutionalizing economic changes. The focus of energy will be on resolving political differences. That focus will produce turmoil, decentralization, professionalization of the military, and a slowdown in economic expansion.

The next several years will be dominated by uncertainty. A violent struggle between central authorities and regional leaders is probable. This struggle will influence the future role of the Communist Party, the military, and business. The party will diminish in importance. The central authorities will have less and less real responsibility. Power will shift to the provinces. The military will undergo a wrenching period of change. In the end it will be more professional and less political. Economic reform will be a victim of all the uncertainty and upheaval that will dominate the Chinese landscape. The economy will not turn back to the prereform days, but neither will there be much progress toward expanded reforms. Instead, economic policy will be an instrument of political competition. The result will be that political interests will become more polarized and more cautious of further change. Promises to protect Hong Kong's autonomy will be an early victim of the polarization and strife that we foresee in China.

❊ 6 ❊

The Future of Hong Kong

Our examination of internal Chinese affairs was discouraging. We could not find reason for optimism. But this still does not explain how life will evolve in Hong Kong. Perhaps China's expected turmoil will result in Hong Kong's being left alone. Possibly China's competing elites will be too busy trying to outmaneuver each other to interfere with activities in Hong Kong. Unfortunately, we do not anticipate such benign neglect. Instead, we think Hong Kong's return to China is likely to contribute to the strife we foresee.

Freedom in the New Hong Kong

Most daily activity is not caught up in politics. People go about their business with little thought about their government. But governments touch on many facets of routine activity. In this chapter we are concerned in part with how routine daily life will be influenced by Hong Kong's transition from Crown Colony to an integral part of the People's Republic of China.

Daily life consists of a thousand small acts. Reading a newspaper, going to school, shopping, investing, listening to campaign speeches, going to court over a minor traffic infraction, and making business deals are just some activities that occupy many of us at one time or another. These activities look very different in free societies from the way they look in controlled societies.

When we pick up a newspaper, the government determines whether we have a choice of information. In societies with a free press, citizens are confident that they get a fairly accurate rendition of events. In societies with a government-controlled press, citizens are more likely to think they are receiving propaganda. They learn to read between the lines, to see what is not said. Few citizens in open societies develop those skills. Hong Kong has long had a free press, but as we discuss in this chapter, our study suggests that freedom of the press is likely to become a thing of the past in Hong Kong.

Whether one is shopping for groceries or signing a multimillion-dollar business deal, government can play a role. In a market economy, the price of giant corporations, just like the price of bread, is determined by competition. Government regulations shape and constrain that competition, sometimes to protect unwary citizens and sometimes to help corrupt politicians or government bureaucrats extract bribes. Hong Kong's greatest asset, besides its industrious people, is its free-market environment. Freedom of commerce, freedom to move capital in and out of Hong Kong, and freedom from substantial government interference in business have helped turn Hong Kong into one of the richest spots in the world. Our analysis suggests that many in China are eager to keep Hong Kong's markets free, but they will be unable to do so.

The foundation of every society is the education of its citizens. A cornerstone of any free society is the free and open exchange of ideas. Nowhere is this more critical than in the realm of education. Where academic freedom is sacrificed to political expedience, innovation and growth cannot persist. Academic freedom ensures that there is competition over ideas just as there must be competition over the price of bread. Take the competition of ideas away, and a society becomes stagnant. That, we believe, is exactly what is in store for Hong Kong in the future. China will not tolerate academic freedom whenever ideas crop up that run counter to the government's concept of what is the best way to run society.

The litany of losses in freedom is a long one. A few items have been touched on. These and several others are examined in depth in this chapter. Together they paint a gloomy picture for the future. We wish we could write an upbeat, optimistic account of Hong Kong's future, but we cannot do so and be faithful to the logic of our method and the evidence we have uncovered.

FREEDOM OF THE PRESS

We begin by examining the prospects of a free press in Hong Kong. Two experts we consulted provided data about the future of the press in Hong Kong. As always, they contributed the basic data about potential influence, policy orientation, and salience for each stakeholder. The data were then analyzed using our model. The analysis paints a frustrating picture for those who value free, independent news media.

Immediately after the return of Hong Kong, the Chinese government will not strictly regulate the press. Instead, it will rely on the news media to police themselves. And, indeed, the press will do so, at first being careful not to report stories that might offend Beijing. There is likely to be a broad consensus for such self-policing within Hong Kong. We predict, however, that after a while, the press will begin to exert more independence. When it does so, the authorities in Beijing will crack down and limit the press. Self-censorship by the press will not be sufficient to satisfy the Chinese authorities.

Self-policing will remain tolerable to the Chinese authorities only for a short time. Then they will pressure business and regional interests to accept a state-directed press. Our study suggests that businessmen in Hong Kong, along with regional business interests, will succumb to that pressure. They will abandon their natural desire for a free press. Jiang Zemin, Li Peng, and the PLA will bully them into tolerating and even endorsing a state-directed press. Presumably, these business and regional interests care about their entrepreneurial opportunities more than they care about this basic freedom.

Interestingly, if there were no international focus on an independent press, Hong Kong residents would enjoy *more* freedom than they will likely retain under world scrutiny. Maintenance of a free media is an important indicator of future developments. Therefore, the United States, the Europeans and, of course, the Taiwanese will keenly watch what China does in Hong Kong. Their attentiveness will precipitate a backlash that would not occur if they ignored this issue. The effects of international pressure can be seen by comparing figures 6.1 and 6.2 (p. 104). In the former, we display our predictions about the evolution of attitudes toward a free press by key Chinese groups in the absence of international pressure. In the latter, we show the anticipated evolution of attitudes toward a free press in the face of external pressure. The outcome without external influence suggests self-censorship, as explained below. The outcome with external pressure suggests virtually no freedom of the press, with provincial interests caving in to pressure from the central leaders in Beijing.

Left to its own devices, the Chinese regime would settle its internal bickering by tolerating moderate self-policing, rather than strict government controls. Figure 6.1 shows key Chinese groups shifting to support a self-policed media if there is no foreign pressure. Self-policing occupies the middle range of the press freedom scale. The PLA and the central party leaders in Beijing, for instance, can be seen in figure 6.1 to change their attitude on press freedom. They start out in favor of a state-controlled press, but agree to tolerate a self-censored media. Without international pressure that forces them to take sides, regional and business interests would not collapse in their quest for a free press. Thus, in this case, and this is the only instance in which we observe this pattern, the international community's involvement will prove harmful. By making

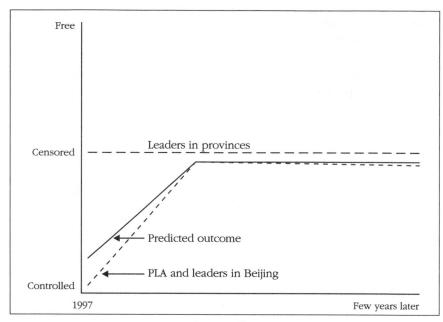

FIGURE 6.1
PRESS FREEDOM WITHOUT FOREIGN PRESSURE

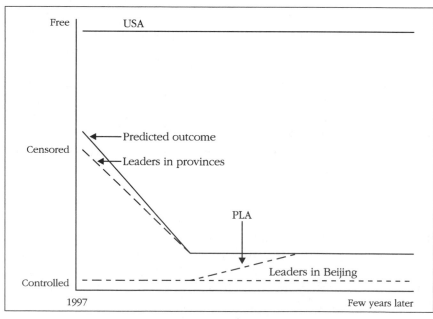

FIGURE 6.2
PRESS FREEDOM WITH FOREIGN PRESSURE

press freedom a cause célèbre, the international community will unify the Chinese opposition.

As can be seen in figure 6.2, central party leaders and the PLA are not prepared to accept self-censorship as the means of controlling the press if foreign pressure is applied. There is too big a risk that they will lose control over the spread of information. What is more, figure 6.2 shows our expectation that the provincial leaders will go along with the hard-line stance that favors state direction of the press if foreign pressure is applied. Apparently, control over the press will be absolutely critical in promoting the perception that things are all right, or at least not too bad, in Hong Kong. Control over the image of Hong Kong conveyed to others seems to be of especially great consequence to political leaders and business interests alike. Therefore, the issue of press freedom will get caught up in the larger question of sovereignty to a greater degree than other freedoms that impinge less directly on access to information by the outside world about how Hong Kong is changing. Once press freedom gets caught up in the question of sovereignty, it is very risky for Chinese interests to side with international sentiment. In this way, the international community unintentionally will increase pressure on internal elements to give up their support for a free press. The tragic consequence is that even self-censorship will cease to be acceptable and the press will become largely a tool of the state.

JUDICIAL FREEDOM

An independent judiciary is a hallmark of a country ruled by law. China has guaranteed that Hong Kong's courts will remain politically independent. Alas, promises all too often are made to be broken. Whether this promise will be kept depends on the international community, which, under the Joint Declaration, has some claim to monitor judicial developments. Chinese authorities, left to their own devices, will make the courts a tool of the political process. They will not preserve or protect an independent judiciary. Unlike press freedom, in this case international involvement is essential to preserve some semblance of the rule of law. This can be readily seen by contrasting figures 6.3 and 6.4 (p. 106). In figure 6.3 we examine how much judicial freedom can be expected if the Chinese regime is unencumbered by foreign pressure. Figure 6.4 shows the effects of foreign pressure, recalling that foreign pressure has legitimacy on this issue with at least some Hong Kong stakeholders because of the international agreements signed between Britain and China. Despite protestations of sovereignty and the difficulties of formally enforcing the international agreements, apparently there is some concern in China not to go too far too quickly. The leaders want to have their cake and eat it too;

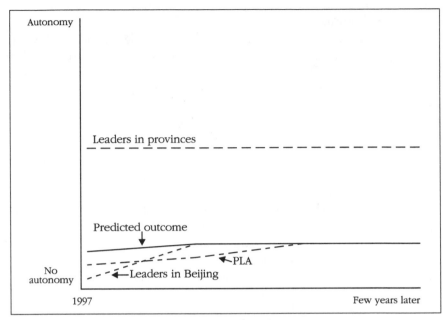

FIGURE 6.3

JUDICIAL INDEPENDENCE WITHOUT FOREIGN PRESSURE

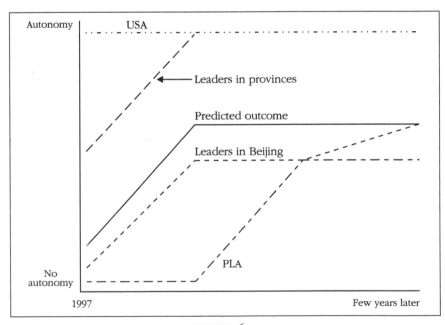

FIGURE 6.4

JUDICIAL INDEPENDENCE WITH FOREIGN PRESSURE

they want to avoid economic repercussions while controlling the courts. They will show some reserve in their grab for control if there is foreign pressure, respecting at least some judicial autonomy in the realm of commercial transactions.

The top of the level of autonomy scale indicates more independence for the judiciary. The mid-range suggests self-policing of the court system and interference by central authorities when political cases arise. The mid-range also indicates that commercial cases will be less encumbered than other matters that come before the courts. The bottom of the scale indicates a Beijing-controlled judiciary.

Plugging the three data sets on the autonomy of the judiciary into the model yielded almost identical conclusions. Although the data from one expert start out by providing a rosy picture, a modest amount of scrutiny reveals a pessimistic pattern similar to what we find in the other two analyses of the judiciary's future.

There is some prospect that the judiciary will enjoy a little independence immediately after 30 June 1997. On sensitive political matters, the Hong Kong courts will defer to Beijing. On commercial matters, they will be left alone. That, at least, is the first impression from our investigation. This impression is bolstered by the fact that this modicum of autonomy enjoys widespread support inside and outside China. But there is a fundamental problem with this picture.

The Chinese government looks upon the role of the judiciary as a strictly internal matter. To put it bluntly, they view the design and function of the court system as their sovereign right. The one problem with their perspective is that they have signed an international agreement guaranteeing the independence of Hong Kong's courts. We have already noted, however, that the international agreement is not binding because it cannot be enforced. Therefore, regardless of international commitments, China is likely to alter Hong Kong's courts to suit its own purposes if it can get away with doing so. Those purposes include making the judiciary a political tool of the state. Those with the most authority in China are also most opposed to any independence for Hong Kong's court system. They may veto any efforts by more progressive forces to maintain any freedom for those courts.

There are two sources of hope for Hong Kong's court system. One is that there are important internal divisions in China over how to treat the courts. The other is that the international community has the leverage to pressure the Chinese government into respecting its commitments on the judicial system. We examine each of these possibilities below, concluding, unfortunately, that they are not likely to save Hong Kong's judiciary.

The leadership in Beijing is adamantly opposed to any independence for the courts, including independence regarding commercial issues. Li Peng, Jiang Zemin, Qian Qichen, and the PLA are unmoved by domestic pressure to grant any independence to the Hong Kong judiciary. That much is evident in figure 6.3. On this issue they are all pursuing their policy satisfaction. Little political gain can be had by changing their stance on the courts. It is not an issue that these politicians can use effectively to improve their competitiveness with one another. Therefore they will not make policy concessions to attract new supporters to their political ambitions. As a result, if they or people like them retain veto authority after 1997, then guarantees of judicial autonomy will be little more than a farce. As long as these national leaders control the appointment of judges, the courts will serve their political interests. The rule of law will be a scarce commodity.

One critical question about the autonomy of the courts, then, is whether the party leaders in Beijing will have veto power over the appointment of judges. The heart of the matter is who will be responsible for the court system in a more decentralized, federalized China? If the center retains control over the courts, we are convinced that the people of Hong Kong can forget any thoughts of an independent judiciary. If the provincial governments gain control over the court system, then Hong Kong has a *chance* of keeping its court system somewhat autonomous. Nevertheless, even some regional elites are opposed to granting such autonomy because they believe it makes it harder for them to compete with Hong Kong. So even the balkanization or confederation of China does not insure the future rule of law in Hong Kong.

The second avenue of hope for judicial autonomy has greater prospects of succeeding *if it is utilized*. Our study shows that international pressure can help muster greater internal Chinese support for judicial independence. In particular, Jiang Zemin and Li Peng are likely to respond positively to sustained international pressure. While they are unresponsive to domestic efforts in support of Hong Kong's judicial system, they are surprisingly responsive to international pressure from the United States, Britain, and the European Union. This is pictured in figure 6.4, where key leadership groups shift dramatically in a relatively short time to give support to more court autonomy. Their initial recalcitrance gives way to a more faithful reflection of the international agreements they have signed. Apparently, they are willing to trade away some of their policy satisfaction for improvement in their *international* political stature.

If international pressure were exerted, the leaders in Beijing would still exercise considerable control over the Hong Kong courts, but they would do so more cautiously and selectively. Li Peng, Jiang Zemin, and their backers would hardly interfere in cases involving business or commercial disputes. They would still pressure judges when important political matters came before the courts. That, of course, still leaves the courts vulnerable to abuses, but it makes such abuses more an exception than the rule.

The international "lobbying" effort needed to protect Hong Kong's judiciary is unlikely to take place. The Chinese will argue that any such international efforts violate their sovereignty. The major sources of possible international pressure, especially the United States, Britain, and the European Union, are expected to back down before they realize how much success they could have in protecting the judicial system in Hong Kong. Thus we do not believe that international pressure will be used successfully on this issue. Instead, after some initial pressure, the future of the judiciary will be left in the hands of China's own leaders. In that case, the Hong Kong court system will be a political tool of the Chinese government. Those who desire autonomous courts for Hong Kong would do well to lobby the American government and others to attend to this issue.

ACADEMIC FREEDOM

The next issue we examine is the future of academic freedom. It is very difficult for a society to remain economically competitive without permitting the free exchange of ideas. To be sure, economic growth can be achieved as long as the society competes on the basis of cheap labor. Academic freedom and its implications for innovation are critical if Hong Kong is to compete successfully in areas where greater skills are required.

We obtained data from three distinguished specialists on this issue. The analysis of two of those three data sets indicate that there is no prospect whatsoever for the continuation of academic freedom in Hong Kong. The analysis based on these two sets of inputs is as pessimistic as can be. We report in depth the analysis of the third expert's data. Those data do not suggest a happy outcome either. They are, however, the most optimistic view revealed in our analysis. That this third pessimistic view is, speaking relatively, the most optimistic is sobering indeed. It too holds out little long-term hope for the free exchange of ideas in Hong Kong.

The preservation of considerable academic freedom could be the consensus point of view for a sustained period. To be sure, the level of such freedom would be reduced from the status quo, but at least the schools would not completely be tools of the state. The prospect of this consensus, however, suffers from two important deficiencies: it is fragile and it depends on sustained international pressure.

The internal Chinese supporters of academic freedom on their own do not have enough clout to persuade or coerce the party hard-liners to permit any academic freedom at all. The future of educational freedom in Hong Kong rests heavily on the fickle attention of international interests in the United States, Taiwan, and elsewhere. If the international pressure wanes, academic freedom will be lost. Our investigation does not encourage optimism that international pressure can be sustained.

Eventually, even if there is continuous international pressure, the consensus for academic freedom will erode. After several years the initial curtailment of such freedom will expand, with support emerging for even more limited academic rights. Educators will be expected to respect the wishes of the central authorities in Beijing. They will not be coerced into doing so right away. Instead, they will understand what the limits of tolerance are and will censor themselves.

Even the modest protection of some academic freedoms will not sit well with the key leaders in Beijing. Indeed, those leaders will veto any effort to maintain academic freedom from the outset if they can. Li Peng, Jiang Zemin, Qian Qichen, and the PLA are adamant in their opposition to such freedom. They are also immovable in their point of view. Despite considerable efforts by others to find a compromise with them, they never relent in their steadfast hostility to academic freedom. They do not want schools to be places where "heretical" ideas are taught or discussed. They and their backers are prepared to go down in a blaze of glory—or should we say ignominy—to prevent the state's loss of control over what is taught. Allowing academic freedom puts their outlook and their political fortunes at risk.

Other important figures in China will seize on the question of academic freedom to bolster their influence *if the international community gives them support*. This is a big "if." Should such support be sustained, academic freedom is likely to be one key element in the anticipated competition between the center and the provinces in China. Although initially reluctant to allow much educational freedom, leaders in Guangdong, Shanghai, and elsewhere outside of Beijing would quickly rally around support for some academic freedom to enhance their own political fortunes. They would use this issue to distinguish themselves from the party's hard-liners and to establish a more liberal image. This would be likely to win for them some new international support in their competition with the central authorities. Their support, then, will be an opportunistic quest for political gains. As our indifference curve analysis indicates, they will sacrifice their policy beliefs for these political benefits, making them poor guarantors of such freedoms once they have achieved their political goals.

The business interests in China, including those that rely on the leaders in Beijing, are also attracted to more openness in schools and universities than would otherwise be their natural inclination. They too are motivated by political (and economic) ambition. A rapidly modernizing country needs access to the latest business techniques and information. Therefore, to continue growth, they can tolerate only those constraints on academic freedom that are unlikely to restrict economic expansion. It is to a large degree their break with the center and their support in the international community that can push the consensus point of view toward preserving some academic freedom. Alas, all of this increased support does not shake the fundamental convictions of the central authorities. As long as they maintain control over the government, academic freedom will be in jeopardy.

The protection or elimination of academic freedom is one of several issues that revolve around the larger question of the regionalization of China, which ultimately is expected to be resolved in favor of regional interests. In the early phases of that struggle, there will be only small erosion in academic freedom as long as the international community stays engaged. Then for a few years there will be retrenchment to harsher treatment for those who express opinions that deviate from the accepted orthodoxy. In the longer term, if the regional interests prevail, there is likely to be a partial restoration of academic freedom compared to what Li Peng or Jiang Zemin would permit. At least the schools would not be so politicized that they stifle all ideas that differ from the party line. As the regional authorities grow in influence, however, they are also likely to backslide. They will want to limit academic freedom again. Remember, they start out being opposed to academic freedom. They prove willing to tolerate some freedom only in the context of international pressure and their competition for control over China's government. Ambition, not conviction, is the source of their support for academic freedom. If they win the competition for control, they are likely to turn back toward their earlier attitudes. They are not expected to go as far as the central party leaders in clamping down on such freedoms, but neither will they allow unfettered rights to be critical of the government. Even under our most optimistic scenario, Hong Kong is expected to enjoy considerably less academic freedom than it knew under the British.

FREE ELECTIONS

What will elections be like in Hong Kong? Regardless of any international scrutiny or international indifference to elections in Hong Kong, such elections will not be free. The United States is very keen to see free elections institutionalized in Hong Kong. To that end, the United States will exert considerable effort. The fruit of its labors will be that China's

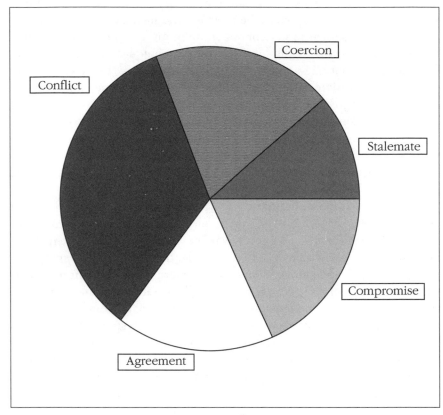

FIGURE 6.5
WILL ELECTIONS BE FREE?

foreign minister will express support for the concept within the inner circles of the Chinese government. The foreign minister's expression of support for free and fair elections will fall on deaf ears.

The electoral process is a divisive issue. The pie chart in figure 6.5 highlights the conflictual nature of the issue. Conflict and coercion make up well over half of the anticipated relations between stakeholders. Among those who do not start out in agreement on the issue, conflict and coercion make up almost two-thirds of all relationships.

Initially, no internal sentiment exists in China for holding free and fair elections. Only one important official eventually gives support to the idea of free elections—the foreign minister. He finds himself in an awkward position. Internal preferences are to manipulate elections for political advantage. He would like elections used in that way as well. External inclinations, however, are to pressure China to hold free elections, at least in Hong Kong. The foreign minister tries to temper international criticism by providing belated support for the concept of free elections. His dramatic shift in position has no effect whatsoever on the sentiments of other Chinese leaders. It may very well mark his political demise. We anticipate that he will find himself embroiled in a costly political conflict, which he probably loses.

The Chinese foreign minister is the only consequential stakeholder expected to move over time toward greater support for free elections. Everyone else either sticks by his initial point of view or moves toward tolerance for less and less freedom in Hong Kong's elections. The winning perspective is to disallow any freedom within the electoral process. The Chinese may go through the motions of holding elections, but the elections will be meaningless.

What can we expect about the political party system, and Hong Kong's chief executive and legislative council? With elections being manipulated by the state, the Chinese authorities will be tolerant of some freedom for political parties. Why not! The elections will be rigged anyway. Whether parties will be active under these conditions is another question, one we do not address. But it will not matter much because whether active or not, they really will not play a role in shaping electoral outcomes.

Chinese officials are sufficiently insecure that, left to themselves, they would ban parties or control them so severely that they would simply be tools of the state. The international community and many in Hong Kong, however, will not allow the Chinese leadership to operate in a vacuum without any semblance of accountability. In the face of external pressure, the Chinese authorities will make concessions regarding political parties. The parties will have a fair amount of freedom to campaign. This can provide a valuable vehicle for getting the message across about China's corruption and disregard for liberty. But that seeming freedom will not translate into electoral influence. On the core issue of political control, the leadership will not grant any rights to Hong Kong. Self-determination will certainly not play a prevalent role in Hong Kong's future. Important electoral determinations will be made by Beijing or by its representatives and backers in Hong Kong.

In whatever direction we look, we see clear evidence that Beijing will control politics in Hong Kong. Not only will elections be rigged, but the chief executive for Hong Kong will be handpicked to do Beijing's bidding. We find that in the early stages after the transition, Beijing will exert substantial control over the chief executive. Still, the individual will have some trappings of apparent independence. To be sure, the trappings will be modest, but they will be there. And why not? The person in the office will have been hand chosen by the central party authorities.

After a couple of years, the chief executive will try to expand the "trappings" of authority, trying to make them into real authority. This will work briefly but will then lead to a severe backlash. By the end of the millennium, Hong Kong's chief executive will have no autonomy at all. He or she will be a servant of and rubber stamp for the political interests in China.

Real interest in an independent chief executive exists only among international observers of the Hong Kong scene. Most stakeholders in Hong Kong would be content with just a modicum of independence for the chief executive. Most stakeholders in Beijing and in China's provinces are intolerant of even that modicum of independence. Ultimately, the hard-line point of view wins.

The picture could be a little brighter for the Legislative Council. Stronger sentiment exists inside Hong Kong for an independent legislature than for an independent chief executive. Perhaps this reflects a realistic viewpoint that suggests Beijing will never permit Hong Kong's executive to be anything other than an agent of the state. We note that optimism about the independence of the legislature must be viewed cautiously. We do find support for the idea that there will be moderate independence. But, of course, this is in a context in which elections are rigged so that many who sit in the chamber will already have been picked by the leaders in China. And even then, the legislature will be a rubber stamp unless international pressure is continually applied to China to compel some respect for it. Left to themselves, as is likely on an issue that goes so directly to the sovereign independence of a state, the Chinese leadership will make the Legislative Council in Hong Kong into a meaningless body much like the legislatures throughout China. Faced with external pressure, however, the legislative council could turn into a place where real debate takes place, even if, in the end, it supports whatever perspective is pushed by the mainland.

A FREE MARKET

For many, especially international businesspeople who are not involved in daily life in Hong Kong, the fundamental question is "Will Hong Kong's market remain free?" Once again we observe a common pattern across expert inputs to our model. All of our assessments support the conclusion that Hong Kong will have a fairly free market after its return to China. Still, the market will not be as free as it is today. Businesses will be expected to monitor their activities, restraining themselves from practices that might embarrass or irritate the authorities in Beijing.

One way in which Hong Kong is of great value to China is as a marketplace to the world. In view of that fact, it is surprising to discover how much resistance there is to keeping the market in Hong Kong really free. Among competing Chinese elites we find a fundamental division. Regional interests favor keeping as free a market as possible. Central authorities, by contrast, want a somewhat more controlled economy. They appear to favor cronyism perhaps along the lines of what prevailed during Marcos's rule in the Philippines. We predict that regional interests will prevail. In doing so, however, they will moderate their initial point of view somewhat. That is, provincial leaders and the leaders at the center will work out some mutual accommodation. The upshot will be some modest government control over the market and some sensitivity to the feelings of the central elite through self-censoring by business. Hong Kong's economic freedom will be somewhat diminished.

The PLA is likely to play an important role in the evolution of Hong Kong's marketplace. This should not come as a great surprise. We have already noted that elements in the PLA have one foot in the center and another in the provinces. They have an especially large stake in the continued economic success of Hong Kong and they also have an eye out for the welfare of the leaders in Beijing. Through their intercession and efforts by others, we anticipate a smooth transition from today's free-market economy to a somewhat more regulated and controlled economy in the future. Hong Kong's growth will probably slow down as a result. The Hong Kong marketplace will be less free than it is now, but it will be considerably freer than the rest of the Chinese economy.

Exactly what sorts of constraints will be introduced into Hong Kong's economy by the Chinese takeover? To address this question, we investigate four aspects of business. One concerns the awarding of contracts on a political basis. The second focuses on the willingness of the Chinese leadership to stamp out corruption. Third is the role of labor unions and fourth is freedom of travel. We find discouraging pictures on the first three fronts and a mixed picture on the last.

Qian Qichen turns out to be the pivotal decision maker when it comes to favoritism in business. Li Peng and Jiang Zemin believe business contracts should be awarded *strictly on the basis of favoritism*. They see no reason to give business to people who are not supportive of the regime. This viewpoint is shared by the PLA and many other elements of China's government. Evidence of the Chinese desire to introduce favoritism as a criterion for the awarding of contracts is already evident. As a punishment for the Jardine Company's decision to redomicile in Bermuda, China long opposed the awarding of the contract for container terminal 9 in Hong Kong harbor to a Jardine's subsidiary. Naturally, those elements, such as the PLA, who are the beneficiaries of contracts granted as political rewards wish to see the practice continued. Qian Qichen is not opposed to continued favoritism. Indeed, his initial point of view is that every reasonable excuse should be used to award contracts to sympathetic businesses. But he starts out with a recognition that blatant favoritism will harm Hong Kong's economy. His initial point of view, however, does not prevail for long.

At first we expect cronyism or favoritism to be hidden behind a veil of good business decisions. Then Qian Qichen's resolve breaks and he begins a long, steady shift in attitude. Along with his shift in outlook, the coalition trying to preserve a modicum of good business practice deteriorates. Qian Qichen shifts only slightly at first, endorsing a bit more cronyism than he thinks is appropriate. Then he slips more and more until eventually he closes ranks with the PLA and the other party leaders. By around 1999 business contracts will be awarded on the basis of political loyalty rather than ability to fulfill the contract. Favoritism will come to rule the day.

The favoritism we predict requires some tolerance of corruption. After all, favoritism is itself a form of corruption. And again the analysis provides a clear and consistent picture. China will declare its opposition to all forms of corruption as part of its ruling image in Hong Kong. That declaration will prove to be an overstatement. Hong Kong will not be dominated by corrupt practices, but the government will engage in corruption when it suits its purposes. The granting of business opportunities to favorites is just one example of the corruption we expect will be tolerated by the Chinese rulers of Hong Kong.

Labor unions will follow a standard pattern for communist states. They will be agencies of the party. As such, they will not represent the interests of workers in the sense that they do in the West. This might prove to be beneficial for the economic climate in Hong Kong in that strikes and work stoppages are unlikely. But it could prove harmful in that labor can be used as part of the campaign of state control over who is awarded contracts, who can fulfill contracts, and with what accompanying level of corruption.

Freedom to travel is certainly essential for a successful market economy. China's leaders are opposed to free travel and would like to stymie it if they can. Still, they are not completely lacking in pragmatism. Faced with international pressure, especially from business interests around the world (as well as within Hong Kong itself), the central authorities are likely to tolerate travel. They will do so reluctantly and will be prepared to clamp down on individuals who use foreign privileges to be "disloyal" to the state. Questions of travel rights will be quite contentious. China's leaders are against free travel; business interests are in favor. The pivotal group will prove to be the Chinese civil servants. They, of course, will bear responsibility for overseeing the distribution of travel documents. They will allow travel, thereby satisfying essential business interests, but they will keep a close watch on who does what and where. In this way they will satisfy the fears of the central party leadership. Hong Kong businessmen will be able to get around, but they will know that their conduct is being monitored.

Unlike so many other issues we have examined, travel is an area where foreign pressure is likely to be real and sustained. We foresee a reduction in freedom of travel as compared to the policy under the British, but we do not foresee a cutback to a severe degree. Here at least is one area of hope for some openness in China to outside influence.

The Level of Autonomy

China has promised to preserve Hong Kong's autonomy. Will it? As with so many other issues, we anticipate deep division between regional and central authorities over how much autonomy to grant to Hong Kong. None in China, however, favor full autonomy for Hong Kong. Left to themselves, the mainland Chinese would work out a compromise in which only a modest level of autonomy would be granted to Hong Kong. Compared to the level predicted in figure 6.6 (p.118), for instance, internal interests alone would settle the matter by giving Hong Kong a fraction of the autonomy it ultimately can expect. International pressure is vitally important in encouraging greater autonomy for Hong Kong. Still, the issue leaves China divided whether there is international pressure or not.

Jiang Zemin and Li Peng are steadfast in their opposition to autonomy, with Li Peng ever so slightly more liberal than Jiang. Key elites in Hong Kong are equally committed to complete autonomy. They lack the clout, however, to carry the day. But they do have some important influence. Qian Qichen shows considerably more flexibility on this issue than do the other central leaders. Although he too starts out being strongly opposed to autonomy for Hong Kong, he responds to local elites who press for autonomy. Naturally, he does not support unfettered autonomy, but a brand of freedom that grants Hong Kong a considerable degree of freedom of action within the confines of the many constraints on the exchange of ideas and information we have already discussed. His concessions are accompanied by considerable bargaining and maneuvering by those with a business interest in Hong Kong's future. This includes several elements of the military as well as the conventional business commu-

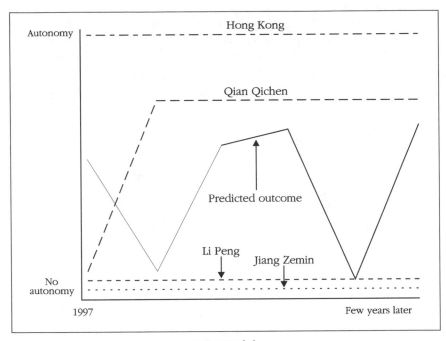

FIGURE 6.6
AUTONOMY FOR HONG KONG

nity. They are all prepared to trade away some autonomy in exchange for a stable and predictable set of rules. And that is what they get, but only after a topsy-turvy competition to define those rules. Figure 6.6 highlights the great uncertainty surrounding the question of Hong Kong's autonomy during the first two years or so after the return to China. Notice how the line depicting our predicted outcome oscillates up and down, signifying the range of choices during 1998 and 1999 more or less. China ultimately will concede some autonomy, but certainly not complete autonomy, to the former Crown Colony. The expected level is seen in figure 6.6 for some later date, perhaps in the year 1999 or 2000. The line denoting the outcome on the issue looks very much like a roller coaster or a roiling ocean. If we were to plot the line beyond the end-point shown on the graph, you would see that it does stabilize at the final level displayed. But getting to that stability is going to involve some rough seas.

Hong Kong is in for a rocky road in the years ahead. Future treatment of Hong Kong will be caught up in the political competition for control of China. Victims of that competition will include the free press, academic freedom, open and fair elections, and some portion of market freedom. Hong Kong will not be as tightly controlled as the rest of China, but neither will it be the free and vivacious place it has been for the past half a century. The political and economic landscape will be filled with uncertainty, cronyism, lost freedoms, and more corruption than has been known in the recent past. It is a bleak picture indeed.

❋ 7 ❋

Fortune Cookies

On 20 August 1995 the Sunday edition of *The New York Times* published an index of corruption in forty-one countries, calculated from surveys of businessmen and journalists. A ranking of 10 would be a place in which no corruption was found and 0 a place in which corruption was perceived to be everywhere. Of the forty-one countries, China had the second lowest score, 2.16. Only Indonesia scored lower. Hong Kong, in marked contrast, had a score of 7.12, midway between Japan's score of 6.72 and the U.S. score of 7.79. Throughout this book we have stated that the most fundamental difference between Hong Kong and China is that Hong Kong is governed by the rule of law, whereas China is subject to the rule of man. The British Crown, Parliament, the common law, and more than a thousand years of tradition have given Hong Kong its key institutions: private property, the rule of law, and minimalist government. Several thousand years of history have given China its key institution: unrestrained rule by a succession of emperors, warlords, and Communist Party autocrats.

A month later, a story headlined "Shanghai Stock Market Cited for Scandal" appeared in the 22 September 1995 edition of *The New York Times*. The author reported that Mr. Wei Wenyuan had been replaced as head of the Shanghai Securities Stock Exchange due to a scandal in the bond futures market. Beginning 23 February 1995, two firms, Shanghai International Securities (Sisco) and the Liaoning Guofa Group, tried to manipulate the market to save themselves from huge losses incurred by betting the wrong way on bond futures. They ignored trading limits and then flouted exchange rules by selling short to drive prices down. The bond futures market was suspended, reopened the following week, and then closed indefinitely in May. The chief executive of Shanghai International resigned in April and was arrested in July on charges of illegally using public funds and embezzlement. It was estimated that his firm lost more than $100 million in a wild day of trading, more than its registered capital. Among Sisco's Hong Kong partners was Cheung Kong, headed by local property tycoon Li Ka-Shing (whose personal assets are in trust somewhere in the West Indies). Some securities analysts in Hong Kong noted that the decision to close the bond futures market shows "how arbitrary decision-making still is in China."

Arbitrariness in China contrasts sharply with certainty in countries governed by the rule of law, as is evident in a huge advertisement that appeared in the 11 September 1995 issue of *Forbes*. Known as Suntec City, a consortium of eleven powerful Hong Kong businessmen, including the very same Li Ka-Shing (Cheung Kong Holdings), along with Cheng Yu-Tong (New World Development Company), and Lee Shau-Kee (Henderson Land Development Company), are investing 2 billion Singapore dollars to develop the largest privately owned commercial development in the island republic. Suntec City will be built on a prime downtown site near Singapore's harbor. It will provide 490,000 square meters of convention, exhibition, office, retail, and entertainment space. This gives meaning to the concept of diversification into "rule of law" domiciles on the part of property tycoons whose fortunes were made in Hong Kong.

On 17 September 1995 Hong Kong held its last election under British rule, but the first in which its Legislative Council was fully elected in a bizarre mixture of directly and indirectly elected seats—twenty general constituency seats, thirty functional constituency seats, and ten seats chosen by the directly elected District Boards. Candidates of the pro-China party, the Democratic Alliance for the Betterment of Hong Kong, including its leader Tsang Yok-Sing, were soundly defeated, winning only six seats. The two prodemocracy, anti-China Democratic and Liberal parties won twenty-nine seats, mostly by margins of 2 to 1 or more. Twenty independent candidates, including many other critics of China, also won easily. Perhaps the only consolation Chinese leaders could take from their stunning defeat was the relatively low turnout of 36 percent of Hong Kong's nearly 3 million registered voters.

One hour after the voting booths opened, China's official New China News Agency reminded Hong Kong voters, as they stood in line to elect their representatives, that China's central government would dismiss in 1997 the candidates the voters were choosing that day. In the perverse logic that is Marxism–Leninism–Mao Zedong–Deng Xiaoping thought, China denounced the election as "unfair and unreasonable." Why? Because pro-China candidates lost badly. These two statements do not bode well for the survival, after 1 July 1997, of liberty or of the bourgeois liberalism feared and hated by mainland leaders.

In the wake of the massacre at Tiananmen Square, the British government offered to make up to 250,000 British passports available to heads of households and their families in Hong Kong. In the course of a BBC radio program in late September 1995, Governor Chris Patten, the architect and leading advocate of Hong Kong's electoral reform, suggested that the colony's 3.4 million British subjects should have the right of abode in Britain. British government officials immediately ruled out the suggestion, and the opposition Labor Party chimed in its support for the Conservative government's immigration policy. To his credit, Governor Patten had voiced, though perhaps a bit late, what many in Hong Kong have long felt was Britain's moral obligation to the people of Hong Kong.

General Warning Signals

The title of this book, *Red Flag over Hong Kong*, sets the tone for the future of Hong Kong. On 1 July 1997 China's flag, five yellow stars on a red background, will be hoisted over Government House, the residence of Hong Kong's chief executive. A second red flag—Hong Kong's new flag, a white bauhinia flower on a red background—will be hoisted alongside the motherland's flag. Perhaps the red flag is a poor choice of symbols. After all, a red flag is a general warning signal of imminent danger. And, in Hong Kong's unique geographical setting, a red flag signals severe typhoon danger.

The gathering storm over Hong Kong presages a turbulent future. Little of what the world has come to associate with Hong Kong will survive intact. China is soon to embark on a wrenching political transition. Party and government officials in Beijing will increasingly share power with leaders in the southern coastal provinces, the Yangzi delta, and other newly emerging economic centers. Energy will be expended in the struggle between those who want money and those who want power. Hong Kong will be a pawn in that conflict.

Business optimists might think that the monied interests want to preserve Hong Kong and its riches to serve China's economic development. Political optimists might think with equal conviction that both Beijing and the regions want to preserve Hong Kong's stability and prosperity to bankroll their quest for power. The boom years of the 1980s seemed to confirm both perspectives. Entrepreneurs argued that Hong Kong was as likely to take over China as was China to take over Hong Kong. Political pundits proclaimed that China would never kill the goose that laid the golden eggs.

The incident at Tiananmen Square terrified both groups. It revealed the truth of Communist Party rule, that the retention and exercise of raw political power takes precedence over all other issues.

China may not kill the golden goose, but it will be so crippled that it will lay fewer and fewer golden eggs. Growing turmoil between regional and central leaders will beget uncertainty, which will retard growth and stymie prosperity. Even as provincial leaders wrest considerable control from the center, it must be said that regional interests do not lie firmly in alliance with Hong Kong. The special administration region is, after all, their chief competitor.

China's central and regional leaders will not conspire to erode Hong Kong's vitality intentionally and systematically. They will not issue edicts against Hong Kong's entrepreneurs or markets or capriciously change economic policies. Indeed, they may even try, at least at first, to live up to the promise of autonomy for Hong Kong clearly stated in the Joint Declaration and Basic Law.

They will fail, however, because they are ill equipped by thinking and experience to manage Hong Kong's vibrant, free-market economy, and they are downright hostile to the personal freedoms that 6 million Hong Kong residents exercise. China's leaders are equipped and pre-pared, first and foremost, to maintain their own power at any cost. Hong Kong's luster will tarnish, perhaps overnight, but more likely through a process of gradual erosion.

Before 30 June 1997, China could take actions or issue edicts that irreparably shatter confidence in Hong Kong. For example, another inci-dent at Tiananmen Square or a break in diplomatic relations with the United States over Taiwan would throw Hong Kong's financial markets into a panic. Neither of these events is likely, but both are possible.

More likely, though still far from certain, China could hasten the de-cline of Hong Kong by statements and measures that undermine the con-fidence of those with money or skills to leave. China could state its plans not to recognize foreign travel documents acquired by Hong Kong-born Chinese. It could announce a strict loyalty test for civil servants. Perhaps most damaging, it could change the linkage of the Hong Kong dollar from the U.S. dollar to the renminbi. Barring a dramatic turn of events, such as an overt power struggle on the mainland, all these measures ap-pear unlikely before 1997.

But China has issued numerous statements and taken several meas-ures that have already eroded a good deal of confidence in Hong Kong's future.

□ China has suggested that the press should practice self-discipline and be especially respectful of sentiments in Beijing. Many Hong Kong journalists will emigrate before 1997. Those who remain will master the art of self-censorship.

□ China has insisted that civil service personnel files be turned over to them. More than a third of the inspectorate level of the Hong Kong police force has indicated an intention to leave, including the man in charge of persuading them to stay. Attrition in the civil service has risen.

□ Chinese naval police abducted Hong Kong seamen in Hong Kong waters in April 1995.

□ A subsidiary of China's aviation regulatory body, China National Aviation Corporation, has applied for a license to operate from the territory. Its ostensible purpose is to compete with Cathay Pacific Airways and Hong Kong Dragon Airlines. An unstated goal is to force a sale of additional shares in Cathay Pacific to Chinese interests at a preferential price to ensure a majority Chinese stake in Cathay.

□ In September 1994 Chinese authorities closed down a research center in China that conducted an unpublished opinion poll that associated Deng Xiaoping with the crackdown on prodemocracy students. The putative excuse was that the institute was improperly registered.

□ In May 1995 the immensely profitable *South China Morning Post* abruptly canceled a popular cartoon strip, "The World of Lily Wong," which had run for eight years. Its author, Larry Feign, frequently ridiculed Chinese communist officials. The column was allegedly dropped as part of a cost-cutting move—by one of the world's most profitable newspapers. Virtually every vacant job is advertised in the *Post*, and it is common to see young Chinese residents of Hong Kong struggling to read English job listings that appear in the *Post*.

□ Jimmy Lai, founder of the highly profitable clothing chain Giordano, was notified that his Beijing branch was closed down for lack of proper registration—shortly after he published a critical column on Deng Xiaoping in his *Next* magazine. Lai subsequently sold his interests in Tiger Enterprises, a joint-venture between Giordano and the mainland, and reduced his stake from 37 percent to 27 percent in Giordano itself, which removed him as the controlling shareholder.

□ Undercover propaganda activity has intensified in New China News Agency in the past ten years. Its staff has quadrupled, few of whom are from Hong Kong. It maintains a "coordination department," which is a political unit to woo support for Chinese policies.

□ In September 1994 a special commentary appeared in the official

People's Daily that called for keeping the national language pure and free of slang. The author decried the infiltration of trendy phrases from Hong Kong in advertising and conversation to show off and said that "speaking the official Mandarin Chinese tongue with a Hong Kong accent was disgusting." The commentary declared that fervent love for and the correct use of the motherland's language are crucial parts of patriotic education.

□ In keeping with Hong Kong's Bill of Rights, several formerly repressive colonial ordinances were amended in Hong Kong. The legal subgroup of the preliminary working committee proposed that these items should be resurrected after 1997. If reinstated, the police would have greater control over public meetings, the territory's chief executive could revoke a television license on the grounds of "security of Hong Kong," the chief executive could review program standards and content of television and radio, and could declare unregistered groups illegal. The subgroup also said that the Bill of Rights would not be superior to any other legislation and that it was not required to take into account the International Covenant on Civil and Political Rights when interpreting the Bill of Rights.

As these episodes demonstrate, China's leaders have deliberately or inadvertently opened Pandora's box from time to time, but they have also managed to close it before too many demons escaped. But each incident weakens confidence in the future of Hong Kong and the liberties of its 6 million people. Still, we believe that China will not deliberately or knowingly precipitate a disaster before 1 July 1997.

When sovereignty over Hong Kong reverts to China, a myriad of decisions will have to be taken. Many have obvious implications for building or destroying confidence in Chinese rule. Others are more subtle but no less consequential. Let us ruminate about these decisions and the flashpoints associated with them.

4 June 1998! Every year, thousands of people have taken to the streets of Hong Kong to demonstrate, before the offices of New China News Agency, in remembrance of those who died at Tiananmen Square. This demonstration will be the ninth. It is nothing new. But now the rulers of Hong Kong are those who ordered tanks to fire on students on 4 June 1989. Will the government of the special administrative region of Hong Kong issue a permit for the demonstration? Will the police block or permit a march? Will the people of Hong Kong fear the consequences of turning out to demonstrate? Will retaliation be taken against any marchers? On 4 June 1998 China's promise of one country, two systems

will be challenged. A crackdown will signal the death knell of autonomy and Hong Kong's liberties. A failure to crack down could ignite similar demonstrations in cities throughout China, as millions clamor for the liberties enjoyed by their Hong Kong compatriots. China's leaders will find themselves between a rock and a hard place.

But 4 June is only one anniversary that will challenge China's commitment to Deng's oft-stated principle of "one country, two systems." The double ten celebration, 10 October, commemorates the founding of the Nationalist government of Sun Yat-sen in China in 1911. Every year, supporters of the Nationalist regime in Hong Kong celebrate this occasion with a large, gala party, which includes flying the Nationalist flag. The government in Beijing regards Taiwan as an integral part of China, but considers Taiwan's rulers to be usurpers. The First of October, the founding date of the People's Republic of China, not 10 October, is the proper date for celebration. Indeed, mainland officials routinely protest the flying of the Nationalist flag in Hong Kong as an affront to their sovereignty. What will they do if one or more Hong Kong residents dare to fly the nationalist flag on 10 October? Flying a flag is a manifestation of free speech, which is promised in the Joint Declaration and Basic Law. But it also is an assault on Beijing's sensitivities. Will the exercise of free speech become synonymous with treasonable "acts of state?"

Celebrations and anniversaries are not the only flashpoints to challenge China's commitments. A host of everyday decisions will signal whether our gloomy story is right or wrong. Consider a seemingly simple choice. Young children in Hong Kong today are educated primarily in Cantonese and English. Who can argue against the idea that national unification would be enhanced if students were educated in Mandarin as their primary language? Cantonese is spoken only in and around Guangdong Province. It is not the primary language of government or business throughout most of China.

A knowledge of Mandarin would better equip Hong Kong's population to play a larger role in China's social and economic development. Fluency in Mandarin would give Hong Kong's people access to all forms of communication emanating from the mainland. Linguistic divisions are a source of friction in many countries—India, Canada, Belgium, to name a few. Language politics is even becoming an issue in the United States. It would be prudent for China's leaders to address this potential problem to minimize its impact in the absorption of Hong Kong.

Mao Zedong understood the importance of language as a unifying principle. Almost immediately after the revolution, he issued orders to simplify hundreds of the most commonly used, complex Chinese characters to increase literacy. He promoted Mandarin, formerly the spoken language of the emperor's officials or the literati, by renaming it *putong-hua*, which means ordinary speech. This principle is likely to be extended to Hong Kong.

Many mainland Chinese schoolchildren, like their counterparts in Hong Kong, study two languages—Mandarin and English. There is no reason for them to learn Cantonese unless they live in Guangdong Province. In that case, they learn Cantonese naturally by hearing it spoken in the home. By learning English, Chinese schoolchildren are given the opportunity to play a role in the growing international business sector that fosters so much of China's overseas trade. Without English, these children will be at a disadvantage when they grow up. If Hong Kong's children are forced to abandon the study of English to learn Mandarin, then they will be at a competitive disadvantage in the future. As future business leaders, those without a knowledge of English will be poorly equipped to engage in international commerce, which is the lifeblood of Hong Kong's economy. By a simple change in language priorities, and for eminently sensible reasons, China could shift competitive business advantages away from Hong Kong to the mainland.

There is evidence already of the erosion of English in Hong Kong and the shift to greater reliance in the colony on mainlanders who speak English. Hong Kong Telecom's directory assistance calls are answered across the border in Guangdong Province. The Hongkong and Shanghai Banking Corporation employs more than 800 mainlanders in branches throughout Hong Kong, in part because of a shortage of local people who speak English.

This shortage reflects the emigration of skilled English speakers from Hong Kong in anticipation of the dreaded date of 1997, when China resumes sovereignty. Too, schools in Hong Kong report a decrease in student interest in English. Students now think that they must learn three languages: Cantonese, Mandarin, and English. With their schedules heavily squeezed, English is the first language to go.

In recent years, the Hong Kong General Chamber of Commerce has sought permission to import as many as 100,000 English-speaking mainlanders to fill positions that require English-language speakers. As the next century unfolds, Hong Kong may regress to the status of a Chinese-speaking coastal city instead of the great international city that it is today.

There is another, equally ominous, portent in the decline of English in Hong Kong. A society with personal freedoms and many English speakers is bound to read Western publications and watch western television programs. English offers a window to a cosmopolitan, free world that is much less accessible to Chinese speakers. Beijing's airport, for instance, is startling for the absence of a news kiosk. Hong Kong's airport teems with every conceivable source of information. As English declines in Hong Kong, it will be easier for the mainland to limit news and information, to control the press, and to determine what people hear, see, and think.

Economic Flashpoints

The most visible flashpoints will be economic—the currency, the stock and property markets, emigration, unemployment, corruption, specific retail sectors, to name a few. In addition to the specific forecasts set out in the two preceding chapters, let's take a careful look at possible warnings signs—red flags as it were—over Hong Kong.

THE HONG KONG DOLLAR

The Hong Kong dollar is, literally, as good as the greenback. Every Hong Kong dollar in circulation is backed by an equivalent value in U.S. dollars in the custody of the Hong Kong government, at a fixed exchange rate of US$1 = HK$7.80. Hong Kong dollars are so sound that a substantial share of them, perhaps a third or more of their outstanding value, circulate outside Hong Kong, mainly in Shenzhen and Guangdong Province.

The Joint Declaration says precisely that "the Hong Kong dollar will continue to circulate and remain freely convertible." The Basic Law, in Article 111, says that "the Hong Kong dollar, as the legal tender in the Hong Kong Special Administrative Region, shall continue to circulate." It further states that "the issue of Hong Kong currency must be backed by a 100 percent reserve fund." Article 112 states that no foreign exchange control policies shall be applied in Hong Kong.

As long as the link to the U.S. dollar remains in force, Hong Kong's post-1997 "constitution" amounts to maintaining the U.S. dollar, one step removed at a rate of $1 = HK$7.80, as the legal tender of a special administration region of the People's Republic of China. The rest of China, meanwhile, functions with a floating-rate renminbi, which is not fully convertible and which is not backed by any underlying real, hard assets apart from the central Chinese government's power to tax.

On 1 July 1997 a newly unified China will have two official currencies: a U.S.-dollar-backed, freely convertible Hong Kong dollar and an extremely volatile, unbacked, possibly inconvertible renminbi. This does not sound like a recipe for long-term internal monetary stability, not to mention that it discriminates against 1.2 billion mainland Chinese who are stuck with the less-desirable renminbi.

But neither the Joint Declaration nor the Basic Law stipulates what assets are to be held in the reserve fund of the Hong Kong special administrative region. Nor does either document state that pre-1997 arrangements shall remain in force after 1997. The new Hong Kong government is bound to maintain a reserve fund; but under the language of both documents, it could shift from U.S. dollars to other currencies or financial assets. There is nothing that would prevent the new government from switching to, say, renminbi, state-issued mainland bonds, or other mainland assets. It could fix a rate between the Hong Kong dollar and the renminbi and then float up and down against other foreign currencies through its link to the renminbi.

The era of post-Deng politics, as the regions claw power from the center, will further strain the stability of the renminbi, which is not much to begin with. As the central party and government leaders lose their ability to tax and conduct monetary policy in the new decentralized Chinese economy, the Hong Kong dollar (remember, it is really the U.S. dollar one step removed) will look increasingly attractive to Chinese residents. Hong Kong's huge dollar reserves, more than $50 billion, may become irresistible to the rival leaders in Beijing, Shanghai, and Canton. If a real or even rumored grab is made for Hong Kong's foreign reserves, there will be an immediate run on the Hong Kong dollar by international currency traders and local residents, as depositors rush to convert Hong Kong dollar holdings into U.S. dollars and other hard foreign currencies. China is not likely to stand idly by and watch billions of dollars of foreign reserves drain from Hong Kong's banks. In the electronic age, money travels amazingly fast. For example, in just one day in the autumn of 1992, known as Sweden's black Friday, $3.5 billion fled the country, an amount equal to three-quarters of the foreign reserves of Sweden's central bank. Convertibility will be the first casualty of a run on the currency, and the fixed exchange rate between the Hong Kong and U.S. dollars will be severed. Or a bank run might provide the excuse to switch the link from the U.S. dollar to the renminbi. A new link with China's national currency would de facto unify the two currencies.

A bank-run scenario is not new. Black Saturday, 24 September 1983, is still fresh in the minds of many Hong Kong people. On that day, in the midst of the acrimonious Sino-British negotiations over the future of Hong Kong, a bank run, along with a run on rice stocks and toilet paper, threatened to bring down the entire financial structure of Hong Kong. The Hong Kong government made contingency plans to declare the U.S. dollar legal tender and arranged with the Federal Reserve Bank of San Francisco to fly in millions of U.S. dollars to stem the bank run. The run ceased when the Hong Kong government announced its plan to link the Hong Kong dollar to the U.S. dollar.

Hong Kong's banks have been free to accept deposits in foreign currencies. Over the years, the composition of deposits has shifted increasingly in favor of foreign currencies. Estimates of capital outflow since the early 1980s are in the billions of dollars, to such places as the Channel Islands, Bermuda, the Cayman Islands, the United States, Canada, Britain, Australia, and other safe havens. Large personal fortunes left Hong Kong years ago, as attested by private money managers and bankers. The middle class is free to move its money and valuables, and no doubt hundreds of thousands of middle-class people are shifting funds abroad in the remaining months before July 1997. Only business assets remain in Hong Kong, and these funds can be quickly shifted offshore at the first sign of currency troubles.

As if to grab a headline two years in advance of the handover, Moody's Investors Service issued a report on Hong Kong's banks in August 1995, stating that they were "well-capitalized, highly liquid and profitable." More important, Moody's said that Hong Kong's regulators were in a stronger position than ever to maintain the local currency's peg to the U.S. dollar. So, stocks and property prices surged? Wrong. Selling hit all markets, and the Hong Kong Monetary Authority intervened to stabilize a falling Hong Kong dollar. The mere fact that Moody's raised the issue of the link, and the possibility of a speculative attack against the Hong Kong dollar with fewer than two years left under British rule, gave financial markets a severe case of jitters.

The Bank of China has put its imprimatur on the Hong Kong dollar. On 1 May 1994 it began to issue Hong Kong banknotes with a picture of its Hong Kong headquarters, a controversial, knife-edged structure designed by world-renowned architect I.M. Pei. The Bank of China also sits on the exchange fund, which decides how to invest Hong Kong's reserves. Its reputation is now, it would seem, inextricably bound up with the stability of the Hong Kong dollar.

But the Bank of China is a Hong Kong branch of the national Bank of China. It has no separate political power and authority apart from that which it is given from the mainland. It could not, and would not, resist a mandate from Beijing to support a change in the composition of Hong Kong's foreign reserves or a switch from the link with the U.S. dollar to some other reserve asset. If George Soros and other currency speculators earned over $1 billion betting against European currencies, the prospects of even larger profits may lure speculators to sell Hong Kong dollars short. If the Hong Kong government appears to waffle in the slightest in its defense of the U.S. dollar link, no one will hold or buy Hong Kong dollars, and the renminbi could well become Hong Kong's new currency.

In the *Far Eastern Economic Review*'s focus on banking in Asia in 1995, bankers in Hong Kong expressed concern about the "possibility of capital flight as 1997 approaches," that "many residents of Hong Kong will close their Hong Kong dollar accounts in Hong Kong banks in the run-up to 30 June 1997," and that 15 percent of local deposits could flee the colony in a worst-case scenario.

The country of domicile is an issue for Hong Kong's big banks once Hong Kong becomes part of mainland China. Why would anyone want to keep large amounts of money in Hong Kong banks when funds would be safer in Singapore? It is a simple fact that there are no financial centers anywhere in the communist world—not in China, North Korea, Vietnam, Cuba, or any of the East bloc transition economies. Even new Russian millionaires salt their money away in the Bahamas, Cyprus, and other offshore centers. If Li Ka-Shing moved all his assets into a trust in the West Indies, why would any Hong Kong Chinese of means leave personal wealth in Hong Kong banks? After all, it is very easy to move as much money into Hong Kong as is necessary to pay business or personal expenses each month.

Finally, there is the issue of mainland Chinese deposits and investments in Hong Kong. Until 1 July 1997, deposits and investments by mainland enterprises in Hong Kong count as foreign assets from China's point of view, and are treated differently from deposits and investments on the mainland proper. Chinese firms—whether owned by private investors, towns and villages, the military, or the central government—receive preferential treatment on their foreign assets. For example, reinvestment of Hong Kong funds back into China, even if owned by a mainland enterprise, is eligible for special tax breaks and other benefits compared with funds invested from purely internal Chinese sources.

What will happen after 1997 when Hong Kong becomes sovereign Chinese territory? Will Hong Kong financial assets continue to enjoy the status of foreign assets, or will they be put on a level playing field with internal Chinese assets? Will mainland Chinese who want to park money offshore trust their fortunes to Hong Kong banks that are now legally domiciled in a special administrative region of China? Will self-interest encourage much of this "hot" mainland money to move to Singapore and other "safe havens?"

The potential scope of financial dislocation is large. Mainland Chinese enterprises have displaced U.S. firms as the single largest source of foreign investment in Hong Kong. Deposits by mainland enterprises make up a substantial portion of Hong Kong dollar liabilities. A rush to the exit by mainland firms seeking to avoid financial controls by Beijing over this money would strain the Hong Kong dollar along with the territory's credit structure. Who more than mainland Chinese are well acquainted with the benefits that Hong Kong, as a foreign territory, has afforded their earnings and assets? Who doubts that many of them will want to preserve that status?

PENSIONS

Wrapped up with the currency is the concern over pensions. Many people in Hong Kong have accumulated substantial pensions and are worried about what will happen to them after 1997. Memories are still fresh over the treatment of Shanghai residents who lost their pensions after the communists seized the city in 1948. The only way any Hong Kong resident can be absolutely, positively certain of obtaining his full pension benefits is to cash them out before 1997 and place the funds offshore for safekeeping. The size and scope of these pensions has not been precisely quantified, but they run in the billions of dollars.

A front-page feature that appeared in late September 1995 in the *South China Morning Post* revealed the high degree of anxiety about pensions. The story noted that Hong Kong has eighty-four government-run secondary and primary schools, each with a principal. At the close of the 1994–95 academic year, fourteen principals retired with full pension benefits and twenty-two simply stood down from their posts. For the 1995–96 academic year, twenty-two principals applied to retire in September 1996. In addition, sixteen principals from what are known as "government-aided" secondary schools plan to emigrate before 1997. This rate of retirement is triple that of the previous six or seven years. Approximately a third of the more than 3,500 teachers who resigned during 1994–95 emigrated, many taking advantage of the British Nationality Selection Scheme.

Prompting this wave of retirements and emigration is the concern of many "that they will be given [Chinese] state bonds instead of money [hard, convertible currency] if they retire after 1997." School administrators also have fresh memories of the Cultural Revolution, the Red Guards Mao unleashed in the late 1960s, that hit educators extremely hard, relegating them to the lowest category, the ninth class of "stinking intellectuals." By September 1996, massive retirements and emigration will mean that only a few principals will have more than four years' experience.

PROPERTY

The flick of a computer screen is sufficient to move millions of dollars anywhere around the globe. It is not so easy to move buildings and land. Much of the personal wealth of Hong Kong's 6 million people is tied up in their apartments. Demand for housing in Hong Kong's booming economy had pushed up the price of even small apartments beyond a million U.S. dollars, and rents as high as $10,000 a month or more for ordinary units. The most important block of equities listed on the Hong Kong Stock Exchange are property shares. Therefore, every new land auction in Hong Kong becomes a heart-stopping event. Every resale of a major office building or prestigious residential address is equally wrenching.

From the beginning of 1991 through the middle of 1994, residential property increased more than 250 percent in price, and office accommodation more than 150 percent. Prices rose more than 30 percent during a feverish scramble for space during the first quarter of 1994 alone. Speculative trading in uncompleted units became frantic. The boom in property reflected an economic boom in China, where annual economic growth rates hit 30 percent in Shenzhen, 20 percent in Guangdong Province, and 15 percent overall in China. Space in Hong Kong became highly desirable. Supply simply could not keep up with demand. The Hang Seng Index quadrupled, from 3,000 in early 1991 to surpass an incredible 12,000 in early 1994.

The markets turned down in mid-1994. Property prices fell sharply, with commercial offices down as much as 30 percent in a few months. Many long-time Hong Kong residents sold their apartments and became renters. Some blamed the rise in U.S. interest rates, which forced up interest rates in Hong Kong because the Hong Kong dollar is linked to its U.S. counterpart. Others blamed the decline in property values on the tightening of credit in mainland China, which reduced the inflow of funds from China into Hong Kong's property market. Still others blamed the decline on oversupply of new commercial premises. Others blamed the decline on the Hong Kong government, which tightened up the procedures for the presale of apartments and its stated intention to make more land available for development. Few blamed 1997, as if the consequences were either irrelevant or too terrible to contemplate.

Land auctions may be the single most-watched economic indicator during the next few years. Land auctions reveal the demand for new residential and commercial development in Hong Kong, and thus expectations about the future health of the economy. They also place a valuation on existing property because in Hong Kong, the cost of land is the largest component in property prices. Indeed, property shares on the stock exchange fell much more quickly in 1994 than the actual decline in real estate values, since property firms must mark down to market value all inventory when land auctions disclose lower valuations. Some Hong Kong property owners and developers even wish that 1997 would come sooner in the hope that mainland firms setting up shop in Hong Kong will give a boost to demand and push prices back up.

This scenario is perhaps more wishful thinking than economic reality. Remember, several hundred thousand middle-class Hong Kong residents might pack their bags in the remaining months before 1997. If they put their apartments or office buildings on the market to raise cash, sellers will overwhelm buyers and the market will clear at sharply lower prices—assuming buyers can be found at all. The departure of foreign residents will reduce the demand for rental accommodations. Foreign residents, especially those of rival Asian nations, are leaving Hong Kong in large numbers, as exemplified in the creation of a "good-bye" column in the newsletter of the Philippine Association to list departures. There have been several prior instances in Hong Kong's modern history when property values fell by two-thirds or more, almost overnight. A sharp decline in property prices would send equity values spiraling downward and pose a strain on the balance sheets of local banks that have lent heavily for property. Bank earnings would shrink, bank share values would fall, and concern about the Hong Kong dollar would increase.

The optimists and wishful thinkers believe that China will not let Hong Kong's land and equity markets collapse precipitously before or shortly after its takeover of the colony. China will prop up land values, if need be, by overbidding for new land at Hong Kong's regular land auctions. In August 1995, for example, CITIC Pacific, the quoted Hong Kong arm of the China International Trust and Investment Company (which reports directly to China's State Council), and its parent paid $435 million, well over market, to buy an old naval dock on which to erect another waterfront skyscraper. If necessary, the local Bank of China will lend whatever funds are required to finance property sales or new development, at least for the next few years. Land auctions will be put on hold if market conditions are not favorable. But not even China has the spare cash to support a property market of all sellers and no buyers, especially if Hong Kong's upper and middle classes head for the exit in droves. Economic and political confidence are fragile in the best of circumstances, and China, as we have noted, has tested that confidence on more than one occasion.

To boost confidence, a group of Hong Kong businessmen with close connections to China set up a foundation in September 1995 aimed at promoting the territory's image ahead of 1997. Twenty trustees of the Better Hong Kong Foundation, including Li Ka-Shing, Lee Shau-Kee, Stanley Ho (Macao gambling magnate), and Sir Run Run Shaw (television and film mogul), have each contributed US$646,500 for a total of about $13 million. The objective of the foundation is to counter the spread of "inaccurate information" through the news media about Hong Kong's transfer to Chinese sovereignty. So why, Hong Kong skeptics ask, did Li Ka-Shing place all his assets in a West Indies trust? Why did he, with Lee Shau-Kee and others, finance the development of Singapore's largest commercial center?

UNEMPLOYMENT

To the envy of the rest of the world, Hong Kong has enjoyed full employment for many years. In 1994, for example, the unemployment rate was 2.3 percent of the labor force. (In most Western industrial democracies, full employment is defined as an unemployment rate of about 5–6 percent. Several Western European countries have double-digit unemployment.) Facing a steep rise in local labor costs during the past decade, Hong Kong entrepreneurs have shifted manufacturing jobs across the border to Shenzhen and Guangdong Province. Job growth in Hong Kong lies in the high value-added services sector, which outnumbers by four-to-one manufacturing jobs in Hong Kong. Indeed, Hong Kong has faced a severe labor shortage in recent years and has imported as many as 25,000 foreign construction workers to engage in reclamation and infrastructure projects, with an additional 17,000 foreign workers to build the new airport. These are in addition to more than 140,000 foreign domestic helpers, mainly Filipinas, who look after the children of Hong Kong's middle class, and nearly 20,000 professionals from sixty countries with specialized technical, administrative, or managerial skills.

The local labor market began to soften in 1995. By fall, the unemployment rate reached 3.5 percent, low by Western standards, but an eleven-year high for Hong Kong. The real fear of Hong Kong residents is not so much a gradual rise in unemployment, but that their future rulers will give their jobs to mainland workers who will be brought into the territory after 1997. Support for the new order may become a political requirement for a job.

ANTIQUES

Tourists and residents alike frequent Hong Kong's antique markets on Cat Street and Hollywood Road. Shop fronts filled with elegant ceramics do a thriving business. But this entire retail trade is at risk after 1997. Hong Kong's porcelain dealers fear that a ban might be placed on the export of Chinese antiques from Hong Kong when Hong Kong is rejoined with the mainland, which would shatter the demand for antiques.

The antique business looms small in the economy of Hong Kong, except to those who earn their living at it. But it points out a potential source of difficulty if and when mainland laws or regulations are applied to Hong Kong. Mainland antique dealers will charge their central government with discriminating in favor of their richer Hong Kong counterparts. Will the central government defend Hong Kong's past practices under the "autonomy" principle, or will it capitulate to local pressure? For how long will the Chinese authorities allow Hong Kong's businessmen to retain their special, unique privileges?

Hong Kong is a duty-free port. It imports almost all of what it sells, and exports almost all of what it produces. Will the tens of thousands of independent business firms in Hong Kong continue to enjoy duty-free imports, as promised in the Joint Declaration and Basic Law, which has made Hong Kong a global emporium, a tourist paradise? Or, under pressure from millions of mainland enterprises, will the central political authorities reduce Hong Kong merchants to the status of their mainland counterparts?

CORRUPTION, CRONYISM, AND FAVORITISM

Deng Xiaoping's economic reforms are often, but mistakenly, characterized as bringing free markets to China. A better description is the term state capitalism. In China, and in its representative Hong Kong branches, the largest businesses are directly under the control of state, provincial, county, or municipal governments. To name a few of the most prominent, CITIC, the Chinese International Trade and Investment Corporation, is under the supervision of the State Council. China Merchants Holding Company is under the Ministry of Communications, China Resources Company is under the Ministry of Foreign Relations and Trade, and China Everbright is controlled by the State Council. At the local level one can find Guangdong Enterprises Limited and Fujian Investment and Enterprise Corporation.

The vice-president of China National Nonferrous Metal Industry Corporation is Deng's son-in-law. The chairman of CITIC Pacific is the son of China's vice-president. The executive director and general manager of CITIC is also the son of a former vice-president. These persons and others, in many cases the children of China's leaders, known as "princelings," have used their positions and influence to gain control of the newly opened economy and have become rich.

Imagine that IBM was a subsidiary of the U.S. Defense Department, that Exxon was controlled by the Commerce Department, R.J. Reynolds by the Department of Health, Education, and Welfare, McDonald Douglas by the U.S. Army, and Bath Shipyards by the U.S. Navy. Imagine that the City of New York owned Consolidated Edison, the local regional electric company, and that Chicago owned hotels, restaurants, and pager services. Finally, try to imagine that the U.S. Coast Guard operated brothels and prostitution rings.

But even this analogy is not the full story. In addition to the major companies being tied to national and regional political interests, we would have to place the sons, daughters, grandsons, and granddaughters of leading political and military families in charge of these firms. For instance, David Eisenhower would run Exxon, Amy Carter would be the chief executive officer of IBM, and Maureen Reagan would manage Consolidated Edison.

The People's Liberation Army will become a major player in Hong Kong real estate after 1997. It will take over valuable sites in prime locations. It will become one of the largest property companies in Hong Kong with a land portfolio worth billions of dollars. The PLA today has as many as 20,000 companies throughout China, and some of them derive the bulk of their revenues from civilian activities. Their activities include such "legal" products as hotels, cellular pagers, and pharmaceuticals. Among their "illegal" activities, the military runs brothels and hijacks freighters in international waters carrying consumer goods. It has been accused of responsibility for almost half of all piracy attacks in the South China Sea.

How widespread is corruption in China? It is endemic. Only the rare case of official corruption is prosecuted, and this is largely for political show. The Chinese term, *guanxi,* which means connections, is a euphemism for corruption, cronyism, or favoritism. But connections are to be expected where there is no rule of law.

Will corruption infect Hong Kong? The Independent Commission Against Corruption, the ICAC, was established in the 1970s. It successfully rooted out endemic corruption in the police force. It is independent of the civil service, and the commissioner is directly responsible to the governor. In 1994, for example, it received more than 3,600 reports alleging corruption, of which about 38 percent were made against civil servants. The ICAC itself is subject to a stringent system of checks and balances to prevent any abuse of power.

The number of cases of corruption has increased as Hong Kong's ties with China have expanded. In one weekend alone, fifteen policemen were arrested on corruption-related charges. In time, Hong Kong will face the dilemma of how to deal with the princelings who settle in Hong Kong and whether it will be allowed to attack high-level abuses.

Political Reforms

We conclude this foray into the future by laying out an immediate political flashpoint—Patten's democratic reforms. If Chinese threats are taken at face value, we already know the following: China will dissolve Hong Kong's elected legislature on 1 July 1997. China will appoint a provisional legislature until new elections are held sometime during the next few years. China will announce a new set of electoral arrangements that ensures its control over that newly-elected legislature (which we forecast in chapter 6).

During the past two years, the Chinese government has floated several trial balloons suggesting that they prefer a form of proportional representation. Proportional representation means that each party receives as many seats as its share of the vote. So, for example, a party that received 10 percent of the vote would get 10 percent of the seats, or six seats in a sixty-seat legislature. Most proportional representation schemes require a minimum fraction of the vote, somewhere between 1 to 3 percent, to qualify for a seat.

For the 1995 election, twenty of the legislature's sixty seats were contested on the basis of geographical constituencies. A total of 911,951 people voted for candidates to fill these twenty seats. If a pure system of proportional representation had been in place for these twenty seats, in place of Patten's arrangements, the outcome would have been substantially different. On the pro-China side, the Democratic Alliance for the Betterment of Hong Kong, which received roughly 29 percent of the total vote and won only two seats, would have won five seats. On the anti-China side, Martin Lee's Democratic Party and independents identified with it, which won 52 percent of the vote and fifteen seats, would have only nine seats. Three parties that won no geographical constituency seats would each have won one seat.

Even if the mainland maintained the electoral arrangements for the other forty seats, a combination of thirty functional constituencies and ten seats chosen by District Boards, the changes in the twenty geographical constituency seats stemming from proportional representation would shift the voting bloc in the legislature from anti-China to pro-China. As of 18 September 1995, the Democrats and their allies appeared to have a two-seat majority (31–29) on their tough-minded approach to dealing with China. But under a proportional representation system, the pro-China Democratic Alliance and its allies would enjoy a comfortable ten-vote edge, 35–25, on issues relating to China. A simple change to proportional representation for twenty of the sixty seats in the legislature could allow mainland-backed politicians to dominate fully the legislative agenda.

Public demonstrations, the language of instruction, the Hong Kong dollar, pensions, property values, antique markets, unemployment, corruption, and electoral reform are just a few of the flashpoints we have addressed. These issues will provide early warning indicators of the core predictions we set forth about the future of Hong Kong and China.

But there are other flashpoints we might also have enumerated. These include the first feared midnight knock on the door, requests of Hong Kong residents to make patriotic charitable contributions to the motherland, appointments of mainland officials to the boards of directors of Hong Kong companies, bargain-basement purchases of stakes in Hong Kong-listed firms by mainland enterprises, green-clothed soldiers of the PLA visibly stationed in Hong Kong's central district, talk of a "get-even" list of those who fled the mainland to live under colonial rule, and so on. The catalog is bound only by the limits of imagination. None of these may every happen; all of them loom in the back of the mind of Hong Kong's residents.

Finally, there is a human element. It stands apart from any formal analysis of political competition and conflict. The "new world order" is one in which more and more countries are abandoning authoritarianism for democracy. Hong Kong is moving in the opposite direction. It is being integrated into an authoritarian regime that has had a history few would care to emulate. Can the Chinese authorities be trusted to honor the Joint Declaration and Basic Law? This is a fair question, given that one of Hong Kong's richest, pro-China residents, Li Ka-Shing, placed his personal wealth in trusts in the West Indies. How will Hong Kong's 6 million residents respond to the actual takeover? Will they remain calm and put their trust to fate? Or will they panic and head for the exit at China's first threatening statement or sign of misconduct? Indeed, is every outbound flight on 30 June 1997 already sold out?

Appendixes

❋ Appendix A ❋

Joint Declaration
of the Government of the United Kingdom
of Great Britain and Northern Ireland
and the Government
of the People's Republic of China
on the Question of Hong Kong

The Government of the United Kingdom of Great Britain and Northern Ireland and the Government of the People's Republic of China have reviewed with satisfaction the friendly relations existing between the two Governments and peoples in recent years and agreed that a proper negotiated settlement of the question of Hong Kong, which is left over from the past, is conducive to the maintenance of the prosperity and stability of Hong Kong and to the further strengthening and development of the relations between the two countries on a new basis. To this end, they have, after talks between the delegations of the two Governments, agreed to declare as follows:

1. The Government of the People's Republic of China declares that to recover the Hong Kong area (including Hong Kong Island, Kowloon and the New Territories, hereinafter referred to as Hong Kong) is the common aspiration of the entire Chinese people, and that it has decided to resume the exercise of sovereignty over Hong Kong with effect from 1 July 1997.

2. The Government of the United Kingdom declares that it will restore Hong Kong to the People's Republic of China with effect from 1 July 1997.

3. The Government of the People's Republic of China declares that

the basic policies of the People's Republic of China regarding Hong Kong are as follows:

(1) Upholding national unity and territorial integrity and taking account of the history of Hong Kong and its realities, the People's Republic of China has decided to establish, in accordance with the provisions of Article 31 of the Constitution of the People's Republic of China, a Hong Kong Special Administrative Region upon resuming the exercise of sovereignty over Hong Kong.

(2) The Hong Kong Special Administrative Region will be directly under the authority of the Central People's Government of the People's Republic of China. The Hong Kong Special Administrative Region will enjoy a high degree of autonomy, except in foreign and defence affairs which are the responsibilities of the Central People's Government.

(3) The Hong Kong Special Administrative Region will be vested with executive, legislative and independent judicial power, including that of final adjudication. The laws currently in force in Hong Kong will remain basically unchanged.

(4) The Government of the Hong Kong Special Administrative Region will be composed of local inhabitants. The chief executive will be appointed by the Central People's Government on the basis of the results of elections or consultations to be held locally. Principal officials will be nominated by the chief executive of the Hong Kong Special Administrative Region for appointment by the Central People's Government. Chinese and foreign nationals previously working in the public and police services in the government departments of Hong Kong may remain in employment. British and other foreign nationals may also be employed to serve as advisers or hold certain public posts in government departments of the Hong Kong Special Administrative Region.

(5) The current social and economic systems in Hong Kong will remain unchanged, and so will the life-style. Rights and freedoms, including those of the person, of speech, of the press, of assembly, of association, of travel, of movement, of correspondence, of strike, of choice of occupation, of academic research and of religious belief will be ensured by law in the Hong Kong Special Administrative Region. Private property, ownership of enterprises, legitimate right of inheritance and foreign investment will be protected by law.

(6) The Hong Kong Special Administrative Region will retain the status of a free port and a separate customs territory.

(7) The Hong Kong Special Administrative Region will retain the status of an international financial centre, and its markets for foreign exchange, gold, securities and futures will continue. There will be free flow of capital. The Hong Kong dollar will continue to circulate and remain freely convertible.

(8) The Hong Kong Special Administrative Region will have independent finances. The Central People's Government will not levy taxes on the Hong Kong Special Administrative Region.

(9) The Hong Kong Special Administrative Region may establish mutually beneficial economic relations with the United Kingdom and other countries, whose economic interests in Hong Kong will be given due regard.

(10) Using the name of "Hong Kong, China," the Hong Kong Special Administrative Region may on its own maintain and develop economic and cultural relations and conclude relevant agreements with states, regions and relevant international organisations. The Government of the Hong Kong Special Administrative Region may on its own issue travel documents for entry into and exit from Hong Kong.

(11) The maintenance of public order in the Hong Kong Special Administrative Region will be the responsibility of the Government of the Hong Kong Special Administrative Region.

(12) The above-stated basic policies of the People's Republic of China regarding Hong Kong and the elaboration of them in Annex I to this Joint Declaration will be stipulated, in a Basic Law of the Hong Kong Special Administrative Region of the People's Republic of China, by the National People's Congress of the People's Republic of China, and they will remain unchanged for 50 years.

4. The Government of the United Kingdom and the Government of the People's Republic of China declare that, during the transitional period between the date of the entry into force of this Joint Declaration and 30 June 1997, the Government of the United Kingdom will be responsible for the administration of Hong Kong with the object of preserving its economic prosperity and social stability; and that the Government of the People's Republic of China will give its cooperation in this connection.

5. The Government of the United Kingdom and the Government of the People's Republic of China declare that, in order to ensure a smooth transfer of government in 1997, and with a view to the effective implementation of this Joint Declaration, a Sino-British Joint Liaison Group

will be set up when this Joint Declaration enters into force; and that it will be established and will function in accordance with the provisions of Annex II to this Joint Declaration.

6. The Government of the United Kingdom and the Government of the People's Republic of China declare that land leases in Hong Kong and other related matters will be dealt with in accordance with the provisions of Annex III to this Joint Declaration.

7. The Government of the United Kingdom and the Government of the People's Republic of China agree to implement the preceding declaration and the Annexes to this Joint Declaration.

8. This Joint Declaration is subject to ratification and shall enter into force on the date of the exchange of instruments of ratification, which shall take place in Beijing before 30 June 1985. This Joint Declaration and its Annexes shall be equally binding.

Done in duplicate at Beijing on   1984 in the English and Chinese languages, both texts being equally authentic.

(Signed)   *(Signed)*

For the Government of the   For the Government of the
United Kingdom of   People's Republic of
Great Britain and   China
Northern Ireland

Annex I.
Elaboration by the Government of the People's Republic of China of Its Basic Policies Regarding Hong Kong

The Government of the People's Republic of China elaborates the basic policies of the People's Republic of China regarding Hong Kong as set out in paragraph 3 of the Joint Declaration of the Government of the United Kingdom of Great Britain and Northern Ireland and the Government of the People's Republic of China on the Question of Hong Kong as follows:

I

The Constitution of the People's Republic of China stipulates in Article 31 that "the state may establish special administrative regions when necessary. The systems to be instituted in special administrative regions shall be prescribed by laws enacted by the National People's Congress in the light of specific conditions." In accordance with this Article, the People's Republic of China shall, upon the resumption of the exercise of sovereignty over Hong Kong on 1 July 1997, establish the Hong Kong Special Administrative Region of the People's Republic of China. The National People's Congress of the People's Republic of China shall enact and promulgate a Basic Law of the Hong Kong Special Administrative Region of the People's Republic of China (hereinafter referred to as the Basic Law) in accordance with the Constitution of the People's Republic of China, stipulating that after the establishment of the Hong Kong Special Administrative Region the socialist system and socialist policies shall not be practiced in the Hong Kong Special Administrative Region and that Hong Kong's previous capitalist system and life-style shall remain unchanged for 50 years.

The Hong Kong Special Administrative Region shall be directly under the authority of the Central People's Government of the People's Republic of China and shall enjoy a high degree of autonomy. Except for foreign and defence affairs which are the responsibilities of the Central People's Government, the Hong Kong Special Administrative Region shall be vested with executive, legislative and independent judicial power, including that of final adjudication. The Central People's Government shall authorise the Hong Kong Special Administrative Region to conduct on its own those external affairs specified in Section XI of this Annex.

The government and legislature of the Hong Kong Special Administrative Region shall be selected by election or through consultations held locally and be appointed by the Central People's Government. Principal officials (equivalent to Secretaries) shall be nominated by the chief executive of the Hong Kong Special Administrative Region and appointed by the Central People's Government. The legislature of the Hong Kong Special Administrative Region shall be constituted by elections. The executive authorities shall abide by the law and shall be accountable to the legislature.

In addition to Chinese, English may also be used in organs of government and in the courts in the Hong Kong Special Administrative Region.

Apart from displaying the national flag and national emblem of the People's Republic of China, the Hong Kong Special Administrative Region may use a regional flag and emblem of its own.

II

After the establishment of the Hong Kong Special Administrative Region, the laws previously in force in Hong Kong (i.e., the common law, rules of equity, ordinances, subordinate legislation and customary law) shall be maintained, save for any that contravene the Basic Law and subject to any amendment by the Hong Kong Special Administrative Region legislature.

The legislative power of the Hong Kong Special Administrative Region shall be vested in the legislature of the Hong Kong Special Administrative Region. The legislature may on its own authority enact laws in accordance with the provisions of the Basic Law and legal procedures, and report them to the Standing Committee of the National People's Congress for the record. Laws enacted by the legislature which are in accordance with the Basic Law and legal procedures shall be regarded as valid.

The laws of the Hong Kong Special Administrative Region shall be the Basic Law, and the laws previously in force in Hong Kong and laws enacted by the Hong Kong Special Administrative Region legislature as above.

III

After the establishment of the Hong Kong Special Administrative Region, the judicial system previously practised in Hong Kong shall be maintained except for those changes consequent upon the vesting in the courts of the Hong Kong Special Administrative Region of the power of final adjudication.

Judicial power in the Hong Kong Special Administrative Region shall be vested in the courts of the Hong Kong Special Administrative Region. The courts shall exercise judicial power independently and free from any interference. Members of the judiciary shall be immune from legal action in respect of their judicial functions. The courts shall decide cases in accordance with the laws of the Hong Kong Special Administrative Region and may refer to precedents in other common law jurisdictions.

Judges of the Hong Kong Special Administrative Region courts shall be appointed by the chief executive of the Hong Kong Special Administrative Region acting in accordance with the recommendation of an independent commission composed of local judges, persons from the legal profession and other eminent persons. Judges shall be chosen by reference to their judicial qualities and may be recruited from other common law jurisdictions. A judge may only be removed for inability to discharge the functions of office, or for misbehaviour, by the chief executive of the Hong Kong Special Administrative Region acting in accordance with the recommendation of a tribunal appointed by the chief judge of the court of final appeal, consisting of not fewer than three local judges. Additionally, the appointment or removal of principal judges (i.e., those of the highest rank) shall be made by the chief executive with the endorsement of the Hong Kong Special Administrative Region legislature and reported to the Standing Committee of the National People's Congress for the record. The system of appointment and removal of judicial officers other than judges shall be maintained.

The power of final judgment of the Hong Kong Special Administrative Region shall be vested in the court of final appeal in the Hong Kong Special Administrative Region, which may as required invite judges from other common law jurisdictions to sit on the court of final appeal.

A prosecuting authority of the Hong Kong Special Administrative Region shall control criminal prosecutions free from any interference.

On the basis of the system previously operating in Hong Kong, the Hong Kong Special Administrative Region Government shall on its own make provision for local lawyers and lawyers from outside the Hong Kong Special Administrative Region to work and practise in the Hong Kong Special Administrative Region.

The Central People's Government shall assist or authorise the Hong Kong Special Administrative Region Government to make appropriate arrangements for reciprocal juridical assistance with foreign states.

IV

After the establishment of the Hong Kong Special Administrative Region, public servants previously serving in Hong Kong in all government departments, including the police department, and members of the judiciary may all remain in employment and continue their service with pay, allowances, benefits and conditions of service no less favourable than before. The Hong Kong Special Administrative Region Government shall pay to such persons who retire or complete their contracts, as well as to those who have retired before 1 July 1997, or to their dependents, all pensions, gratuities, allowances and benefits due to them on terms no less favourable than before, and irrespective of their nationality or place of residence.

The Hong Kong Special Administrative Region Government may employ British and other foreign nationals previously serving in the public service in Hong Kong, and may recruit British and other foreign nationals holding permanent identity cards of the Hong Kong Special Administrative Region to serve as public servants at all levels, except as heads of major government departments (corresponding to branches or departments at Secretary level) including the police department, and as deputy heads of some of those departments. The Hong Kong Special Administrative Region Government may also employ British and other foreign nationals as advisers to government departments and, when there is a need, may recruit qualified candidates from outside the Hong Kong Special Administrative Region to professional and technical posts in government departments. The above shall be employed only in their individual capacities and, like other public servants, shall be responsible to the Hong Kong Special Administrative Region Government.

The appointment and promotion of public servants shall be on the basis of qualifications, experience and ability. Hong Kong's previous system of recruitment, employment, assessment, discipline, training and management for the public service (including special bodies for appointment, pay and conditions of service) shall, save for any provisions providing privileged treatment for foreign nationals, be maintained.

V

The Hong Kong Special Administrative Region shall deal on its own with financial matters, including disposing of its financial resources and drawing up its budgets and its final accounts. The Hong Kong Special Administrative Region shall report its budgets and final accounts to the Central People's Government for the record.

The Central People's Government shall not levy taxes on the Hong Kong Special Administrative Region. The Hong Kong Special Administrative Region shall use its financial revenues exclusively for its own purposes and they shall not be handed over to the Central People's Government. The systems by which taxation and by which there is accountability to the legislature for all public expenditure, and the system for auditing public accounts shall be maintained.

VI

The Hong Kong Special Administrative Region shall maintain the capitalist economic and trade systems previously practised in Hong Kong. The Hong Kong Special Administrative Region Government shall decide its economic and trade policies on its own. Rights concerning the ownership of property, including those relating to acquisition, use, disposal, inheritance and compensation for lawful deprivation (corresponding to the real value of the property concerned, freely convertible and paid without undue delay) shall continue to be protected by law.

The Hong Kong Special Administrative Region shall retain the status of a free port and continue a free trade policy, including the free movement of goods and capital. The Hong Kong Special Administrative Region may on its own maintain and develop economic and trade relations with all states and regions.

The Hong Kong Special Administrative Region shall be a separate customs territory. It may participate in relevant international organisations and international trade agreements (including preferential trade arrangements), such as the General Agreement on Tariffs and Trade and arrangements regarding international trade in textiles. Export quotas, tariff preferences and other similar arrangements obtained by the Hong Kong Special Administrative Region shall be enjoyed exclusively by the Hong Kong Special Administrative Region. The Hong Kong Special Administrative Region shall have authority to issue its own certificates of origin for products manufactured locally, in accordance with prevailing rules of origin.

The Hong Kong Special Administrative Region may, as necessary, establish official and semi-official economic and trade missions in foreign countries, reporting the establishment of such missions to the Central People's Government for the record.

VII

The Hong Kong Special Administrative Region shall retain the status of an international financial centre. The monetary and financial systems previously practised in Hong Kong, including the systems of regulation and supervision of deposit taking institutions and financial markets, shall be maintained.

The Hong Kong Special Administrative Region Government may decide its monetary and financial policies on its own. It shall safeguard the free operation of financial business and the free flow of capital within, into and out of the Hong Kong Special Administrative Region. No exchange control policy shall be applied in the Hong Kong Special Administrative Region. Markets for foreign exchange, gold, securities and futures shall continue.

The Hong Kong dollar, as the local legal tender, shall continue to circulate and remain freely convertible. The authority to issue Hong Kong currency shall be vested in the Hong Kong Special Administrative Region Government. The Hong Kong Special Administrative Region Government may authorise designated banks to issue or continue to issue Hong Kong currency under statutory authority, after satisfying itself that any issue of currency will be soundly based and that the arrangements for such issue are consistent with the object of maintaining the stability of the currency. Hong Kong currency bearing references inappropriate to the status of Hong Kong as a Special Administrative Region of the People's Republic of China shall be progressively replaced and withdrawn from circulation.

The Exchange Fund shall be managed and controlled by the Hong Kong Special Administrative Region Government, primarily for regulating the exchange value of the Hong Kong dollar.

VIII

The Hong Kong Special Administrative Region shall maintain Hong Kong's previous systems of shipping management and shipping regulation, including the system for regulating conditions of seamen. The specific functions and responsibilities of the Hong Kong Special Administrative Region Government in the field of shipping shall be defined by the Hong Kong Special Administrative Region Government on its own. Private shipping businesses and shipping-related businesses and private container terminals in Hong Kong may continue to operate freely.

The Hong Kong Special Administrative Region shall be authorised by the Central People's Government to continue to maintain a shipping register and issue related certificates under its own legislation in the name of "Hong Kong, China."

With the exception of foreign warships, access for which requires the permission of the Central People's Government, ships shall enjoy access to the ports of the Hong Kong Special Administrative Region in accordance with the laws of the Hong Kong Special Administrative Region.

IX

The Hong Kong Special Administrative Region shall maintain the status of Hong Kong as a centre of international and regional aviation. Airlines incorporated and having their principal place of business in Hong Kong and civil aviation related businesses may continue to operate. The Hong Kong Special Administrative Region shall continue the previous system of civil aviation management in Hong Kong, and keep its own aircraft register in accordance with provisions laid down by the Central People's Government concerning nationality marks of aircraft. The Hong Kong Special Administrative Region shall be responsible on its own for matters of routine business and technical management of civil aviation, including the management of airports, the provision of air traffic services within the flight information region of the Hong Kong Special Administrative Region, and the discharge of other responsibilities allocated under the regional air navigation procedures of the International Civil Aviation Organisation.

The Central People's Government shall, in consultation with the Hong Kong Special Administrative Region Government, make arrangements providing for air services between the Hong Kong Special Administrative Region and other parts of the People's Republic of China for airlines incorporated and having their principal place of business in the Hong Kong Special Administrative Region and other airlines of the People's Republic of China. All Air Service Agreements providing for air services between other parts of the People's Republic of China and other states and regions with stops at the Hong Kong Special Administrative Region and air services between the Hong Kong Special Administrative Region and other states and regions with stops at other parts of the People's Republic of China shall be concluded by the Central People's Government. For this purpose, the Central People's Government shall take account of the special conditions and economic interests of the Hong Kong Special Administrative Region Government. Representatives of the Hong Kong Special Administrative Region Government may participate as members of delegations of the Government of the People's Republic of China in air service consultations with foreign governments concerning arrangements for such services.

Acting under specific authorisations from the Central People's Government, the Hong Kong Special Administrative Region Government may:

— renew or amend Air Service Agreements and arrangements previously in force; in principle, all such Agreements and arrangements may be renewed or amended with the rights contained in such previous Agreements and arrangements being as far as possible maintained;

— negotiate and conclude new Air Service Agreements providing

routes for airlines incorporated and having their principal place of business in the Hong Kong Special Administrative Region and rights for overflights and technical stops; and
— negotiate and conclude provisional arrangements where no Air Service Agreement with a foreign state or other region is in force.

All scheduled air services to, from or through the Hong Kong Special Administrative Region which do not operate to, from or through the mainland of China shall be regulated by Air Service Agreements or provisional arrangements referred to in the paragraph.

The Central People's Government shall give the Hong Kong Special Administrative Region Government the authority to:

— negotiate and conclude with other authorities all arrangements concerning the implementation of the above Air Service Agreements and provisional arrangements;
— issue licences to airlines incorporated and having their principal place of business in the Hong Kong Special Administrative Region;
— designate such airlines under the above Air Service Agreements and provisional arrangements; and
— issue permits to foreign airlines for services other than those to, from or through the mainland of China.

X

The Hong Kong Special Administrative Region shall maintain the educational system previously practised in Hong Kong. The Hong Kong Special Administrative Region Government shall on its own decide policies in the fields of culture, education, science and technology, including policies regarding the educational system and its administration, the language of instruction, the allocation of funds, the examination system, the system of academic awards and the recognition of educational and technological qualifications. Institutions of all kinds, including those run by religious and community organisations, may retain their autonomy. They may continue to recruit staff and use teaching materials from outside the Hong Kong Special Administrative Region. Students shall enjoy freedom of choice of education and freedom to pursue their education outside the Hong Kong Special Administrative Region.

XI

Subject to the principle that foreign affairs are the responsibility of the Central People's Government, representatives of the Hong Kong Special

Administrative Region Government may participate, as members of delegations of the Government of the People's Republic of China, in negotiations at the diplomatic level directly affecting the Hong Kong Special Administrative Region conducted by the Central People's Government. The Hong Kong Special Administrative Region may on its own, using the name "Hong Kong, China," maintain and develop relations and conclude and implement agreements with states, regions and relevant international organisations in the appropriate fields, including the economic, trade, financial and monetary, shipping, communications, touristic, cultural and sporting fields. Representatives of the Hong Kong Special Administrative Region Government may participate, as members of delegations of the Government of the People's Republic of China, in international organisations or conferences in appropriate fields limited to states and affecting the Hong Kong Special Administrative Region, or may attend in such other capacity as may be permitted by the Central People's Government and the Organisation or conference concerned, and may express their views in the name of "Hong Kong, China." The Hong Kong Special Administrative Region may, using the name "Hong Kong, China," participate in international organisations and conferences not limited to states.

The application to the Hong Kong Special Administrative Region of international agreements to which the People's Republic of China is or becomes a party shall be decided by the Central People's Government, in accordance with the circumstances and needs of the Hong Kong Special Administrative Region, and after seeking the views of the Hong Kong Special Administrative Region Government. International agreements to which the People's Republic of China is not a party but which are implemented in Hong Kong may remain implemented in the Hong Kong Special Administrative Region. The Central People's Government shall, as necessary, authorise or assist the Hong Kong Special Administrative Region Government to make appropriate arrangements for the application to the Hong Kong Special Administrative Region of other relevant international agreements. The Central People's Government shall take the necessary steps to ensure that the Hong Kong Special Administrative Region shall continue to retain its status in an appropriate capacity in those international organisations of which Hong Kong participates in one capacity or another. The Central People's Government shall, where necessary, facilitate the continued participation of the Hong Kong Special Administrative Region in an appropriate capacity in those international organisations in which Hong Kong is a participant in one capacity or another, but of which the People's Republic of China is not a member.

Foreign consular and other official or semi-official missions may be established in the Hong Kong Special Administrative Region with the approval of the Central People's Government. Consular and other official missions established in Hong Kong by states which have established formal diplomatic relations with the People's Republic of China may be maintained. According to the circumstances of each case, consular and other official missions of states having no formal diplomatic relations with the People's Republic of China may either be maintained or changed to semi-official missions. States not recognised by the People's Republic of China can only establish non-governmental institutions.

The United Kingdom may establish a Consulate-General in the Hong Kong Special Administrative Region.

XII

The maintenance of public order in the Hong Kong Special Administrative Region shall be the responsibility of the Hong Kong Special Administrative Region Government. Military forces sent by the Central People's Government to be stationed in the Hong Kong Special Administrative Region for the purpose of defence shall not interfere in the internal affairs of the Hong Kong Special Administrative Region. Expenditure for these military forces shall be borne by the Central People's Government.

XIII

The Hong Kong Special Administrative Region Government shall protect the rights and freedoms of inhabitants and other persons in the Hong Kong Special Administrative Region according to law. The Hong Kong Special Administrative Region Government shall maintain the rights and freedoms as provided for the laws previously in force in Hong Kong, including freedom of the person, of speech, of the press, of assembly, of association, to form and join trade unions, of correspondence, of travel, of movement, of strike, of demonstration, of choice of occupation, of academic research, of belief, inviolability of the home, the freedom to marry and the right to raise a family freely.

Every person shall have the right to confidential legal advice, access to the courts, representation in the courts by lawyers of his choice, and to obtain judicial remedies. Every person shall have the right to challenge the actions of the executive in the courts.

Religious organisations and believers may maintain their relations with religious organisations and believers elsewhere, and schools, hospitals and welfare institutions run by religious organisations in the Hong Kong Special Administrative Region and those in other parts of the People's Republic of China shall be based on the principles of non-subordination, non-interference and mutual respect.

The provisions of the International Covenant on Civil and Political Rights and the International Covenant on Economic, Social and Cultural Rights as applied to Hong Kong shall remain in force.

XIV

The following categories of persons shall have the right of abode in the Hong Kong Special Administrative Region, and, in accordance with the law of the Hong Kong Special Administrative Region, be qualified to obtain permanent identity cards issued by the Hong Kong Special Administrative Region Government, which state their right of abode:

— all Chinese nationals who were born or who have ordinarily resided in Hong Kong before or after the establishment of the Hong Kong Special Administrative Region for a continuous period of 7 years or more, and persons of Chinese nationality born outside Hong Kong of such Chinese nationals;

— all other persons who have ordinarily resided in Hong Kong before or after the establishment of the Hong Kong Special Administrative Region for a continuous period of 7 years or more and who have taken Hong Kong as their place of permanent residence before or after the establishment of the Hong Kong Special Administrative Region, and persons under 21 years of age who were born of such persons in Hong Kong before or after the establishment of the Hong Kong Special Administrative Region;

— any other persons who had the right of abode only in Hong Kong before the establishment of the Hong Kong Special Administrative Region.

The Central People's Government shall authorise the Hong Kong Special Administrative Region Government to issue, in accordance with the law, passports of the Hong Kong Special Administrative Region of the People's Republic of China to all Chinese nationals who hold permanent identity cards of the Hong Kong Special Administrative Region, and travel documents of the Hong Kong Special Administrative Region of the People's Republic of China to all other persons lawfully residing in the Hong Kong Special Administrative Region. The above passports and documents shall be valid for all states and regions and shall record the holder's right to return to the Hong Kong Special Administrative Region.

For the purpose of travelling to and from the Hong Kong Special Administrative Region, residents of the Hong Kong Special Administrative Region may use travel documents issued by the Hong Kong Special Administrative Region Government, or by other competent authorities of the People's Republic of China, or of other states. Holders of permanent identity cards of the Hong Kong Special Administrative Region may have this fact stated in their travel documents as evidence that the holders have the right of abode in the Hong Kong Special Administrative Region.

Entry into the Hong Kong Special Administrative Region of persons from other parts of China shall continue to be regulated in accordance with the present practice.

The Hong Kong Special Administrative Region Government may apply immigration controls on entry, stay in and departure from the Hong Kong Special Administrative Region by persons from foreign states and regions.

Unless restrained by law, holders of valid travel documents shall be free to leave the Hong Kong Special Administrative Region without special authorisation.

The Central People's Government shall assist or authorise the Hong Kong Special Administrative Region Government to conclude visa abolition agreements with states or regions.

Annex II.
The Sino-British Joint Liaison Group

1. In furtherance of their common aim and in order to ensure a smooth transfer of government in 1997, the Government of the People's Republic of China and the Government of the United Kingdom have agreed to continue their discussions in a friendly spirit and to develop the cooperative relationship which already exists between the two Governments over Hong Kong with a view to the effective implementation of the Joint Declaration.

2. In order to meet the requirements for liaison, consultation and the exchange of information, the two Governments have agreed to set up a Joint Liaison Group.

3. The functions of the Joint Liaison Group shall be:

(a) to conduct consultations on the implementation of the Joint Declaration;
(b) to discuss matters relating to the smooth transfer of government in 1997;
(c) to exchange information and conduct consultations on such subjects as may be agreed by the two sides.

Matters on which there is disagreement in the Joint Liaison Group shall be referred to the two Governments for solution through consultations.

4. Matters for consideration during the first half of the period between the establishment of the Joint Liaison Group and 1 July 1997 shall include:

(a) action to be taken by the two Governments to enable the Hong Kong Special Administrative Region to maintain its economic relations as a separate customs territory, and in particular to ensure the maintenance of Hong Kong's participation in the General Agreement on Tariffs and Trade, the Multifibre Arrangement and other international arrangements; and

(b) action to be taken by the two Governments to ensure the continued application of international rights and obligations affecting Hong Kong.

5. The two Governments have agreed that in the second half of the period between the establishment of the Joint Liaison Group and 1 July 1997 there will be need for closer cooperation, which will therefore be intensified during that period. Matters for consideration during this second period shall include:

(a) procedures to be adopted for the smooth transition in 1997;

(b) action to assist the Hong Kong Special Administrative Region to maintain and develop economic and cultural relations and conclude agreements on these matters with states, regions and relevant international organisations.

6. The Joint Liaison Group shall be an organ for liaison and not an organ of power. It shall play no part in the administration of Hong Kong or the Hong Kong Special Administrative Region. Nor shall it have any supervisory role over that administration. The members and supporting staff of the Joint Liaison Group shall only conduct activities within the scope of the functions of the Joint Liaison Group.

7. Each side shall designate a senior representative, who shall be of Ambassadorial rank, and four other members of the group. Each side may send up to 20 supporting staff.

8. The Joint Liaison Group shall be established on the entry into force of the Joint Declaration. From 1 July 1988 the Joint Liaison Group shall have its principal base in Hong Kong. The Joint Liaison Group shall continue its work until 1 January 2000.

9. The Joint Liaison Group shall meet in Beijing, London and Hong

Kong. It shall meet at least once in each of the three locations in each year. The venue for each meeting shall be agreed between the two sides.

10. Members of the Joint Liaison Group shall enjoy diplomatic privileges and immunities as appropriate when in the three locations. Proceedings of the Joint Liaison Group shall remain confidential unless otherwise agreed between the two sides.

11. The Joint Liaison Group may by agreement between the two sides decide to set up specialist sub-groups to deal with particular subjects requiring expert assistance.

12. Meetings of the Joint Liaison Group and sub-groups may be attended by experts other than the members of the Joint Liaison Group. Each side shall determine the composition of its delegation to particular meetings of the Joint Liaison Group or sub-group in accordance with the subjects to be discussed and the venue chosen.

13. The working procedures of the Joint Liaison Group shall be discussed and decided upon by the two sides within the guidelines laid down in this Annex.

Annex III.
Land Leases

The Government of the United Kingdom and the Government of the People's Republic of China have agreed that, with effect from the entry into force of the Joint Declaration, land leases in Hong Kong and other related matters shall be dealt with in accordance with the following provisions:

1. All leases of land granted or decided upon before the entry into force of the Joint Declaration and those granted thereafter in accordance with paragraphs 2 or 3 of this Annex, and which extend beyond 30 June 1997, and all rights in relation to such leases shall continue to be recognised and protected under the law of the Hong Kong Special Administrative Region.

2. All leases of land granted by the British Hong Kong Government not containing a right of renewal that expire before 30 June 1997, except short term tenancies and leases for special purposes, may be extended if the lessee so wishes for a period expiring not later than 30 June 2047 without payment of an additional premium. An annual rent shall be charged from the date of extension equivalent to 3 per cent of the rateable value of the property at that date, adjusted in step with any changes

in the rateable value thereafter. In the case of old schedule lots, village lots, small houses and similar rural holdings, where the property was on 30 June 1984 held by, or, in the case of small houses granted after that date, the property is granted to, a person descended through the male line from a person who was in 1898 a resident of an established village in Hong Kong, the rent shall remain unchanged so long as the property is held by that person or by one of his lawful successors in the male line. Where leases of land not having a right of renewal expire after 30 June 1997, they shall be dealt with in accordance with the relevant land laws and policies of the Hong Kong Special Administrative Region.

3. From the entry into force of the Joint Declaration until 30 June 1997, new leases of land may be granted by the British Hong Kong Government for terms expiring not later than 30 June 2047. Such leases shall be granted at a premium and nominal rental until 30 June 1997, after which date they shall not require payment of an additional premium but an annual rent equivalent to 3 per cent of the rateable value of the property at that date, adjusted in step with changes in the rateable value thereafter, shall be charged.

4. The total amount of new land to be granted under paragraph 3 of this Annex shall be limited to 50 hectares a year (excluding land to be granted to the Hong Kong Housing Authority for public rental housing) from the entry into force of the Joint Declaration until 30 June 1997.

5. Modifications of the conditions specified in leases granted by the British Hong Kong Government may continue to be granted before 1 July 1997 at a premium equivalent to the difference between the value of the land under the previous conditions and its value under the modified conditions.

6. From the entry into force of the Joint Declaration until 30 June 1997, premium income obtained by the British Hong Kong Government from land transactions shall, after deduction of the average cost of land production, be shared equally between the British Hong Kong Government and the future Hong Kong Special Administrative Region Government. All the income obtained by the British Hong Kong Government, including the amount of the above-mentioned deduction, shall be put into the Capital Works Reserve Fund for the financing of land development and public works in Hong Kong. The Hong Kong Special Administrative Region Government's share of the premium income shall be deposited in banks incorporated in Hong Kong and shall not be drawn on except for the financing of land development and public works in Hong Kong in accordance with the provisions of paragraph 7 (d) of this Annex.

7. A Land Commission shall be established in Hong Kong immedi-

ately upon the entry into force of the Joint Declaration. The Land Commission shall be composed of an equal number of officials designated respectively by the Government of the United Kingdom and the Government of the People's Republic of China together with necessary supporting staff. The officials of the two sides shall be responsible to their respective governments. The Land Commission shall be dissolved on 30 June 1997.

The terms of reference of the Land Commission shall be:

(a) to conduct consultations on the implementation of this Annex;
(b) to monitor observance of the limit specified in paragraph 4 of this Annex, the amount of land granted to the Hong Kong Housing Authority for public rental housing, and the division and use of premium income referred to in paragraph 6 of this Annex;
(c) to consider and decide on proposals from the British Hong Kong Government for increasing the limit referred to in paragraph 4 of this Annex;
(d) to examine proposals for drawing on the Hong Kong Special Administrative Region Government's share of premium income referred to in paragraph 6 of this Annex and to make recommendations to the Chinese side for decision.

Matters on which there is disagreement in the Land Commission shall be referred to the Government of the United Kingdom and Government of the People's Republic of China for decision.

8. Specific details regarding the establishment of the Land Commission shall be finalised separately by the two sides through consultations.

Memoranda
(*To Be Exchanged Between the Two Sides*)

MEMORANDUM

In connection with the Joint Declaration of the Government of the United Kingdom of Great Britain and Northern Ireland and the Government of the People's Republic of China on the question of Hong Kong to be signed this day, the Government of the United Kingdom declares that, subject to the completion of the necessary amendments to the relevant United Kingdom legislation:

(a) All persons who on 30 June 1997 are, by virtue of a connection with Hong Kong, British Dependent Territories citizens (BDTCs) under the law in force in the United Kingdom will cease to be BDTCs with effect from 1 July 1997, but will be eligible to retain an appropriate status which, without conferring the right of abode in the United Kingdom, will entitle them to continue to use passports issued by the Government of the United Kingdom. This status will be acquired by such persons only if they hold or are included in such a British passport issued before 1 July 1997, except that eligible persons born on or after 1 January 1997 but before 1 July 1997 may obtain or be included in such a passport up to 31 December 1997.

(b) No person will acquire BDTC status on or after 1 July 1997 by virtue of a connection with Hong Kong. No person born on or after 1 July 1997 will acquire the status referred to as being appropriate in sub-paragraph (a).

(c) United Kingdom consular officials in the Hong Kong Special Administrative Region and elsewhere may renew and replace passports of persons mentioned in subparagraph (a) and may also issue them to persons, born before 1 July 1997 of such persons, who had previously been included in the passport of their parent.

(d) Those who have obtained or been included in passports issued by the Government of the United Kingdom under subparagraphs (a) and (c) will be entitled to receive, upon request, British consular services and protection when in third countries.

MEMORANDUM

The Government of the People's Republic of China has received the memorandum from the Government of the United Kingdom of Great Britain and Northern Ireland dated 1984.

Under the Nationality Law of the People's Republic of China, all Hong Kong Chinese compatriots, whether they are holders of the "British Dependent Territories citizens' Passport" or not, are Chinese nationals.

Taking account of the historical background of Hong Kong and its realities, the competent authorities of the Government of the People's Republic of China will, with effect from 1 July 1997, permit Chinese nationals in Hong Kong who were previously called "British Dependent Territories citizens" to use travel documents issued by the Government of the United Kingdom for the purpose of travelling to other states and regions.

The above Chinese nationals will not be entitled to British consular protection in the Hong Kong Special Administrative Region and other parts of the People's Republic of China on account of their holding the above-mentioned British travel documents.

❉ Appendix B ❉

The Forecasting Model and Its Track Record

The so-called expected utility model described here represents an example of *applied* modeling. It is a tool designed for practical application. It is concerned with explaining how policy positions of competing interests evolve over time. It leads to predictions about policy outcomes and identifies strategic opportunities for altering expected outcomes. As such, it can be used by scholars to explain and predict decisions about politics at any level of analysis. It can also be used by policymakers and business people to anticipate outcomes and to reshape them to be more in line with their own interests.

The model described here has been more fully discussed in Bruce Bueno de Mesquita and Frans Stokman's *European Community Decision Making* (New Haven: Yale University Press, 1994). Readers interested in a more thorough grounding in this model should consult that source and others identified in its bibliography.

The Logic of the Model

The model used in our study of China and Hong Kong focuses on the application of Duncan Black's median voter theorem and a theorem about the monotonicity between certain expectations and the escalation of political disputes suggested by Bruce Bueno de Mesquita and David Lalman and proved by Jeffrey Banks. The conjunction of these theorems plus concepts from bargaining theory foster the development of a quasi-dynamic political model that includes detailed expectations about agreements or compromises that various "players" or "stakeholders" are willing to make over time and implications of those compromises for the ultimate resolution of the issues in question.

Two constraints are assumed to facilitate prediction and explanation: that issues are unidimensional, so that preferences can be represented on a line segment; and that preferences (and associated utilities) for potential outcomes diminish steadily the farther in Euclidean distance a possible settlement is from a player's preferred outcome. These two constraints are requirements of Black's median voter theorem. That theorem demonstrates that the outcome desired by the median voter is the winning position under the constraints just assumed provided a simple majority is required for victory. Of course, we do not assume that all interesting political problems involve voting. Rather, we assume that the exercise of power by mobilizing resources is the nonvoting analog of votes in most political interactions.

The expected utility model deviates from the median voter theorem in one important way. Black assumed that all voters cast votes and that they do so strictly according to their preferences over the alternatives. This is a natural way to look at decision making in democratic systems. However, Black's theorem has much to tell us in nonvoting situations as well. In applying the median voter theorem to these other settings we must recognize that not everyone is free to "vote" by acting in accordance with his or her preferences among outcomes. Black's theorem did not allow for the possibility that votes are coerced. In most political settings, coercion is a distinct possibility. The expected utility model discussed here recognizes this. It allows for the possibility that some decision makers are compelled to throw their support behind an alternative that they prefer less than some other choice that they can contemplate. Through coercion, it is possible for players to "cross over" the median voter position to back an outcome farther from their true wishes than is the outcome of choice for the median voter. This creates the possibility that the median voter outcome can shift over time even though new voters neither enter nor leave the system.

Banks's monotonicity theorem provides a basis for predicting when policy debates are expected to produce negotiated settlements or, contrarily, to lead to an escalation of friction between competing interests. The monotonicity theorem highlights an important feature of all politics. It tells us that the more one expects to gain from challenging a rival issue position, the more likely one is to undertake the challenge. This simple statement turns out to have interesting and sometimes surprising implications for political intercourse. In particular, Banks's monotonicity result provides part of the theoretical basis for the introduction of coercion into spatial analysis. It offers insights into how to expand the analysis of decision making into arenas in which rational actors can be compelled to back policies that in a less constrained environment they would prefer to oppose.

Using the monotonicity result and the median voter theorem, we suggest a fairly simple model of perceptions and expectations. That model helps us comprehend bargaining and shapes an understanding of the conditions that can lead to a negotiation's becoming excessively conflictual or breaking down. We capitalize on the perceptual features of the proposed model by using comparative static techniques to describe the process by which negotiations unfold, moving from one set of circumstances (and outcomes) to another and yet another.

The model itself depicts a game in which players simultaneously make proposals and exert influence on one another. They then evaluate options and build coalitions by shifting positions on the issue in question. The above steps are repeated sequentially until the issue is resolved. In the game, each player knows three factors: the *potential power* and *policy position* of each player on each issue examined and the *salience* each player associates with each issue. The players (decision makers) do not know how much each other player values alternative outcomes or what perceptions others have about their risks and opportunities. Each player makes choices based on his or her perceptions and expectations, with these perceptions and expectations sometimes proving to be in error.

Let $N = \{i, j, k, \ldots, n\}$ be the set of players (stakeholders) trying to influence a multilateral decision. A player might be a government representative, an official from a faction within a political party or a bureaucracy, a leader of some interest group, an influential private citizen, and so forth.

Let $M = \{a, b, c, \ldots, h\}$ be the set of issues in a multilateral negotiation, and let R_a be the line segment that describes the unidimensional policy continuum for any individual issue a selected from among the larger set of issues M.

Let each player i, $i \in N$, have its own *preferred* resolution of issue a denoted as x_{ia}^*.[1] For any feasible proposed outcome on issue a, say k's proposal, x_k, i's utility for x_k, $u^i x_k$, is a decreasing function of the distance between the proposal and i's preferred resolution, so that $u^i x_k = f(-|x_k - x_i^*|)$. This means that proposals farther from player i's pre-

---

1. x_{ia}^* is the outcome player i has revealed to be preferred on issue a. It may or may not be i's true ideal point. We generally do not know for sure what another player's true ideal point is because there are strategic incentives for a player to misrepresent his or her ideal point. Because the model as applied here assesses policy decisions one issue at a time, we drop the issue-denoting subscript (a, b, etc.) from the notation so that henceforth x_i^* is the preferred position of player i on the issue being evaluated at the moment.

ferred outcome are of less value to i than are proposals closer to i's preferred outcome.

Of infinitely many possible proposals to resolve some issue a, how are we to predict which will be chosen? To answer this question, let us first learn a little more about each player (decision maker) i. In this analysis, each player is endowed with three characteristics. Each player attaches some *utility* to each possible outcome on issue a, as already noted. Each player participating in the bargaining process is also endowed with the *power* to exert some influence over decisions. Let c_{ia} be the capabilities (or power) that player i could bring to bear on issue a, such that the sum of the capabilities of the players in a multilateral decision-making setting is 1.[2] c_i is, then, player i's share of the total *potential* influence that could be brought to bear in the negotiations over some issue a. Each player attaches his own priorities, or *salience*, to the issues that must be confronted. Thus, i may attach considerable importance to issue a and considerably less importance to issue b. Denote the salience of issue a for player i as s_{ia}, with $0 < s_{ia} \leq 1$.[3] Each player is characterized by the values of $u^i x_k$, for all i, $k \in N$, c_i, and s_i on each issue. Any aggregation of individuals with identical values on all three of these variables can constitute a single player (stakeholder) for the purposes of this model. Differences on the available pool of resources or on preferred outcomes or on salience mean that the individuals do not constitute a single group.

It is worth noting that players are defined only by the three characteristics of policy preference, capabilities, and salience. This means that a player can be an individual, a group, an entire nation, a bloc of allies, an international organization, or any collectivity in between. In that sense, this model is quite generic; it is equally applicable to interpersonal decision making, group decision making, and interstate interactions. Its application recognizes no level-of-analysis restrictions.

When alternative courses of action are pitted against each other, the array of forces on either side often determines victory. Of course, this array depends on more than the relative power of the competing interests.

---

2. Again we drop the a subscript from the notation throughout, but the reader is alerted to the fact that the model does not assume that a player's capabilities or potential power is the same on all issues.

3. s_i is assumed to be greater than zero because if it were equal to zero for more than one player (stakeholder) then it is possible for division by zero to arise in the computation of the model. Strictly speaking, then, the model can tolerate one player with a salience of zero. Still, this is an odd concept in that it implies that there is a stakeholder who does not care at all about the issue in question. A player i for whom $s_{ia} = 0$ does not have a stake in the decision.

It depends also on the intensity with which each player prefers one proposed settlement (say j's, $u^i x_j$) to another (say k's, $u^i x_k$) and the willingness to spend influence on the issue in question (s_i)—a budget constraint. Thus, each group has a total number of potential "votes" equal to its capabilities, a factor which may be influenced by external considerations and/or by the institutional arrangements that provide structural constraints on the decision making process. Where structural constraints are relevant, as in GATT decision making, qualified majority voting in the European Union, congressional voting following a presidential veto, Security Council choices, and the like, the model can be readily adapted by changing its key decision rule—the median voter rule—to reflect the operative rule in the situation.

The "votes" cast by player i in a choice between alternatives x_j and x_k are said to equal v_{ia}^{jk}, where

$$(v_{ia}^{jk} \mid x_j, x_k) = (u^i x_j - u^i x_k)(c_i)(s_i). \tag{1}$$

Equation (1) states that the "vote" or power mobilized by player i in a choice between two alternatives (x_j and x_k) is equal to how much i prefers one proposal to the other ($u^i x_j - u^i x_k$) discounted by the potential capabilities of i and by how important the issue is to i (i.e., s_i). The "voting" scheme reflects, if you like, what takes place inside the "smoke-filled room" before the formal, visible decision-making process occurs. It assumes that any formal process echoes the agreements reached beforehand. Put somewhat differently, the model assumes that players engage in a backward induction. They anticipate how the formal decision making setting will influence the action and pick proposals in the smoke-filled room that they believe will survive the formal process. They anticipate future action in the immediately next stage of decision making. They are bounded in their rationality, however, in that they are unable in this model to look farther ahead than the next stage of decision making. So their choices are locally rational but may turn out to be inefficient two or more steps down the road.

The prospect that a proposal will succeed is assumed to depend on how much support can be mustered in its favor against the feasible alternatives. In the expected utility model this is calculated as the sum of "votes" across all players in a comparison between x_j and x_k. This sum equals v^{jk} with

$$v^{jk} = \sum_{i=1}^{n} v_i{}^{jk}. \tag{2}$$

A value of v^{jk} greater than zero implies that x_j defeats x_k because the tacit coalition in favor of j's proposal is more motivated and powerful than the coalition supporting k's proposal. If v^{jk} is less than zero, x_j is expected to be defeated by x_k; and if v^{jk} equals zero, the competing interests are collectively indifferent between the two alternatives.

In any negotiation, there are likely to be many more than two proposed settlements. By pitting all alternatives against one another two at a time, the policy position preferred by the median voter (weighted by intensity of preference, power, and salience) is found. Barring perceptions or beliefs that lead players to switch their position, the median voter position is the predicted outcome (Black 1958). In the original version of the expected utility model, the median voter position was always the predicted outcome; however, the current version allows players to switch positions in response to proposals and pressures from one another. By doing so, the model now incorporates a quasi-dynamic element.

In practice, perceptions or beliefs often lead players to grant concessions or to give in to an opponent's point of view, sometimes even needlessly. Such concessions or capitulations can change the location of the median voter. For now we note only that the initial median voter position can be the predicted outcome provided key players do not switch positions in a way that alters the spatial location of the median voter on the issue continuum. Of course, it is crucial to provide an accounting of when such switches in position are expected to take place.

The initial median voter position is not the final prediction of the model. The beliefs and perceptions of the relevant players frequently suggest compromises and concessions that one or another player is willing to pursue and that other players are willing or compelled to accept. These beliefs and perceptions may influence the array of interests sufficiently to necessitate reestimating the spatial location of the median voter, perhaps several times, until perceptions and positions stabilize around the "dominant" outcome. In order to undertake such *before-the-fact* analytic updating, it is necessary first to develop the means to estimate the relevant beliefs and perceptions.

Perceptual Analysis

The forecasting element of the model reveals what players (decision makers) should expect if everyone acts sincerely in accordance with his or her underlying preferences. What, however, can a player do if the predicted issue outcome is not to his or her liking? Are there strategic maneuvers that can improve the expected outcome?

It is possible and indeed likely that players will engage in private, so-phisticated deals to rearrange the prospective resolution of a controversial issue. These deals may be the result of cooperation and coordination among a subset of players (stakeholders) or they may be the product of conflict and coercion. When the deals are produced by coordination among players, the "deal making" reflects the essence of negotiations. The perceptual model guides inquiries so as to facilitate understanding which "deals" are feasible and which are not; in that way it points out the means to construct the dominant outcome or other, strategically so-phisticated approaches to resolving a policy issue.

If an interest group (player) is dissatisfied with the *expected* out-come, there are essentially four courses of action by which the group (the focal group) might improve its prospects. The group player's leadership can

(i)   alter its own level of effort (i.e., change s_i);
(ii) shift its revealed position, selecting x_i such that $u^i x_i^* \neq u^i x_i$;
(iii) influence those who are willing or can be compelled to make concessions to the focal group so that those players alter their level of effort (i.e., s_k); or
(iv) influence those who are willing or can be compelled to make concessions to the focal group so that those players alter their revealed position x_k so that $u^h x_k^* \neq u^h x_k$.

Here we focus only on point (iv), maneuvers that involve persuading or coercing other groups to switch positions, with the direction and magnitude of any changes in position being dictated by the logic behind the model. Changes in salience are treated analogously.

Players (decision makers) interested in ascertaining what leverage they can exert could benefit from estimating the beliefs held by each other player. To do so requires a focus on the three characteristics—$u^i x_j$ for all $i, j \in N$, s_i, c_i—used to estimate each player's expected utility from challenging or not challenging the policy proposal backed by each potential opponent and for approximating the expected utility that each player i believes its opponent expects to derive from challenging or not challenging the policy goals of player i. In the model envisioned here, players are assumed to calculate the expected consequences of challenging (represented by d) or not challenging (represented by $\sim d$) with alternative proposals. The expected utility for i of not challenging opponent j's policy position or proposing an alternative is denoted as $E^i u^i \Delta x_j | \sim d$. This expected utility is estimated by projecting what player i believes is likely to happen in the absence of the exertion of pressure on an opponent to effect a change in the opponent's issue position. One of three contingencies may arise: player i may expect that, with some probability (Q^i), opponent j is the type that will not alter its current policies over the time period of concern to i, giving player i whatever utility $(u^i\Delta x_j^*|\sim d)$ it receives by preserving the status quo between itself and j; i may expect that j's issue position will change, in which case there is some probability (T^i) that, from i's perspective, the policies of j will get better (with $u^i\Delta x_j^+|\sim d$ being the associated utility) or get worse $(u^i\Delta x_j^-|\sim d)$—so that $u^i\Delta x_j^+|\sim d > u^i\Delta x_j^*|\sim d > u^i\Delta x_j^-|\sim d$. Player i's expected utility if i leaves j's proposal unchallenged is described as

$$E^i u^i\Delta x_j|\sim d = Q^i u^i\Delta x_j^*|\sim d \tag{3}$$
$$+ (1-Q^i)[T^i u^i\Delta x_j^+|\sim d + (1-T^i)u^i\Delta x_j^-|\sim d]$$

Player i can challenge j's position on issue a by proposing a change in j's position. In doing so, i presumably takes into account the probability that j does not care enough $(1-s_j)$ about the issue to resist the settlement proposed by i. Player i also considers the possibility that j will resist i's proposal (s_j), in which case there is some probability (P^i) that i will succeed in enforcing its wishes on j and some probability $(1-P^i)$ that it will fail. Should i succeed, then i will derive the utility associated with compelling or convincing j to switch from its current policy stance to the policy stance supported by i. This is denoted by $u^i\Delta x_j^+|d$, which equals $u^i(x_i-x_j)$. Should i fail, then i confronts the prospect of having to abandon its objectives in favor of those pursued by j, denoted by $(u^i\Delta x_j^-|d) = u^i(x_j-x_i)$. The expected utility for challenging j's proposed resolution of the multilateral dispute, $E^i u^i\Delta x_j|d$, is

$$E^i u^i\Delta x_j|d = s_j(P^i[u^i\Delta x_j^+|d] + (1-P^i)[u^i\Delta x_j^-|d]) \tag{4}$$
$$+ [1-s_j][u^i\Delta x_j^+|d]$$

so that the overall expected utility of i with respect to j's outlook on issue a is

$$E^i u^i\Delta x_j = E^i u^i\Delta x_j|d - E^i u^i\Delta x_j|\sim d \tag{5}$$

Equations (3) and (4) reflect each player's effort to look ahead and estimate the consequences of alternative actions. The difference between the two initial actions—challenge or no challenge—is represented in equation (5). If equation (5) is greater than zero, then i believes that challenging j's position is superior to not challenging it and so i is assumed to make a proposal of its own. If equation (5) is less than zero, then not challenging is preferred and i is said to be deterred. If equation (5) equals zero, then i is indifferent between challenging and not challenging j's proposed settlement. Each player evaluates equation (5) vis-à-vis each other player. In doing so, players take the expected actions of third parties into account. The estimates of P^i, the subjective probability that i will be successful, include calculations of how i expects all other parties to respond to a dispute between i and j over policy settlements. In particular, P^i places each other player in i's coalition, j's coalition, or in a neutral position as indicated by each third party's preference for i's policy proposal or j's. Player j makes a comparable calculation (as does each $k \in N$). Because equation (5) includes such subjective elements as utilities and subjective probabilities, it is possible to estimate a complete matrix of expected utilities that captures all possible confrontations, compromises, and capitulations among all the players participating in the relevant political arena.

Once the expected utility values are estimated, we can denote each relationship between pairs of players (stakeholders). If equation (5) is positive for i and negative for j, then the relationship implies either compromise or coercion. If the value of equation (5) for i is greater than the absolute value of equation (5) as calculated for j, then both players agree that i has the upper hand. In this instance, j is expected to be willing to offer concessions to i, although the concessions are not likely to be as large as i would like. The likely resolution of their exchange is a compromise reflecting the weighted average of i's expectations and j's. If equation (5) is positive for i and negative for j and the absolute value of equation (5) from j's point of view is larger than the value of equation (5) from i's perspective, then j is compelled to accept i's wishes unless someone else offers j an enforceable compromise that spares j from having to capitulate to i. If both i and j believe that they have the upper hand in the relationship, then conflict is likely and that conflict has an uncertain outcome. In the context of international disputes, Bueno de Mesquita has shown that this situation is highly correlated with the probability of a war. Should both i and j believe that equation (5) is negative for them, then there may be blustering and bluffing, but the relationship is expected to be a stalemate. The most likely outcome is that the status quo will continue to prevail between i and j.

Estimating the Model

The various components of equation (5) must each be quantified if the model is to have practical value. The quantification procedures are explained in considerable detail elsewhere, including our 1985 book and Bueno de Mesquita and Stokman's 1994 book, so here we provide only brief, summary descriptions of the methods used for estimating each of the key variables.

The estimation of the subjective probability of success for i in a competition with j is accomplished as follows:

$$P^i = \frac{\sum\limits_{k\,|\,u^k x_i > u^k x_j} |v_k^{ij}|}{\sum\limits_{k=1}^{n} |v_k^{ij}|} \text{ for all } k \in N. \tag{6}$$

The probability measure has its origins in earlier theoretical work on third-party choices during disputes. Altfeld and Bueno de Mesquita reported in 1979 a high rate of accuracy in predicting third-party decisions to join ongoing wars on one side or the other based on a model that yields an expression that is virtually identical to the numerator in the term for estimating P^i. The denominator simply normalizes the value in the numerator so that the overall term falls in the interval (0,1). The numerator and denominator have straightforward political interpretations. The numerator calculates the support i can expect to receive in a confrontation with j. This support depends upon the capabilities of each player who prefers i's policy objective to j's. But capabilities alone are not sufficient information to estimate the value of each third party's support. The capabilities are diminished by the degree to which the issue in question lacks salience for the player whose support level is being estimated. The lower a player's salience score, the less likely that player is to spend resources on the issue in question because it is not an issue of much concern. Finally, the capabilities must also be discounted by the intensity of the player's preference for the outcomes under contention. If a third party is just about indifferent between supporting what i wants and supporting what j wants, then that third party is not likely to put much effort behind helping i win. If, however, a player intensely favors i's objective over j's, then it uses more of its capabilities to help i. Thus, the numerator captures the expected level of support for i. The denominator then reflects the sum of the support for i and for j so that the overall expression reflects the gambling odds for i.

The probability calculation is subjective in that i's estimate of i's chances for success may be quite different from j's estimate of the same value. The subjective component is introduced through the use of estimates of the individual risk-taking profiles of each player. In particular, the utilities for the specific proposals (e.g, x_i, $x_j \in R_a$) that enter into the calculation of v_k are evaluated so that

$$u^i x_j = 1 - |x_i - x_j|^{r_i} \qquad (7)$$

with r_i, the indicator of risk-taking propensities, estimated as described below.

The risk-taking component is fairly complex. It is explained in detail in Bueno de Mesquita and Stokman and only summarized here. The risk indicator estimates the size of the tradeoff made by each player between pursuing political satisfaction and policy satisfaction. By political satisfaction we mean the desire to be seen as a deal maker, as an essential member of the winning coalition, even if that means backing an outcome that the player does not like. By policy satisfaction we mean supporting a substantive policy outcome close to the player's preferred choice, even if that means losing to an inferior choice. In the expected utility model we assume that all players trade off at some rate between the pursuit of policy goals and the pursuit of political goals. (We have explained this tradeoff using indifference curve analysis in chapter 5.)

The security derived from being a deal maker is, of course, a central concept in much of politics, but what does it mean in this context? The closer in expected utility terms a player's public position is on a policy issue to the median voter position, the more secure and the more risk averse the player is. The median voter position is the most secure location on a unidimensional continuum with majority rule, whether that majority is votes or power. After all, the key characteristic of the median voter position is that in head-to-head competition it beats all alternatives. Therefore, the decision to locate close to the median voter in expected utility terms seems to reflect a fear of vulnerability or a tendency to be risk averse. This presumption of risk aversion follows from the notion that the player has chosen a position that minimizes threats to its security at the expense of pursuing the policy it really wants. The farther the player's expected utility score is from being at its possible maximum (while remaining within the feasible set of alternative proposals), the more risk acceptant the player is presumed to be. Algebraically, the risk calculation is

$$R_i = \frac{2\sum_{j=1}^{n} E^i u^i \Delta x_j \; - \; \sum_{j=1}^{n} E^i u^i \Delta x_j(\max) \; - \; \sum_{j=1}^{n} E^i u^i \Delta x_j(\min)}{\sum_{j=1}^{n} E^i u^i \Delta x_j(\max) \; - \; \sum_{j=1}^{n} E^i u^i \Delta x_j(\min)}$$

and

$$r_i = \frac{1 - \dfrac{R_i}{3}}{1 + \dfrac{R_i}{3}},$$

so that r_i ranges between .5 and 2.

The measure of risk taking provides one perspective on how much each player (decision maker) appears to have exchanged political satisfaction (security) for policy goals, or vice versa. The risk-taking measure thus provides a basis for estimating the value attached to the status quo. The first term in the numerator of the main expression for estimating risks is equal to the security and policy value of player i's actual or "real" position—the status quo for the player—while the next two terms place the "real" value within the boundaries of what could have been attained in terms of security or policy. These three values—the actual expected utility, the maximum feasible expected utility, and the minimum feasible expected utility—can be estimated. They evaluate three levels of political satisfaction: the one realized by the player, the most the player could have realized, and the least. Because we already have estimated utilities or satisfaction on the policy dimension, those utilities plus these three security scores provide sufficient information to plot estimated indifference curves.

Utilities for the marginal gains ($u^i \Delta x_j^+ | d$ and $u^i \Delta x_j^+ | {\sim}d$) or losses ($u^i \Delta x_j^- | d$ and $u^i \Delta x_j^- | {\sim}d$) from shifts to alternative proposals are evaluated, using the basic building block just described, in the manner delineated in Bueno de Mesquita and Lalman's *War and Reason* (New Haven: Yale University Press, 1992) and in accordance with equation (7). The expressions $u^i \Delta x_j^+ | {\sim}d$ and $u^i \Delta x_j^- | {\sim}d$ are approximated by comparing the value player i attaches to the current median voter prediction to the value i attaches to the median anticipated if i accepts j's proposed policy outcome.

Equation (5) is estimated from four perspectives, with relevant superscripts on equation (5) indicating from whose perspective the calculation is being viewed:

(1) i's expected utility vis-à-vis each opponent j's proposal;
(2) i's perception of each j's expected utility vis-à-vis i's proposal;
(3) j's expected utility vis-à-vis each i's proposal; and
(4) j's perception of each i's expected utility vis-à-vis j's proposal.

The expected utility values summarized in (1) and (2) and in (3) and (4) respectively describe each player's perception of its relationship vis-à-vis each other player. With Banks's monotonicity of escalation theorem in mind, these relationships can be described in continuous form. According to Banks's theorem, the probability with which a player anticipates confronting a given opponent increases with the expected utility of challenging the opponent's proposal, so that the higher some player *i*'s expected utility is with regard to persuading some other player *j* to accept *i*'s position, the greater the likelihood that *i* will confront *j*.

The likelihood that confrontation or concessions will occur can be displayed in a polar coordinate space as in figure B.1. For ease of presentation, we divide such a space into six sectors, their boundaries reflecting fundamental turning points in the probability functions. Figure B.1 displays such a space, labeling each of the six sectors to reflect the

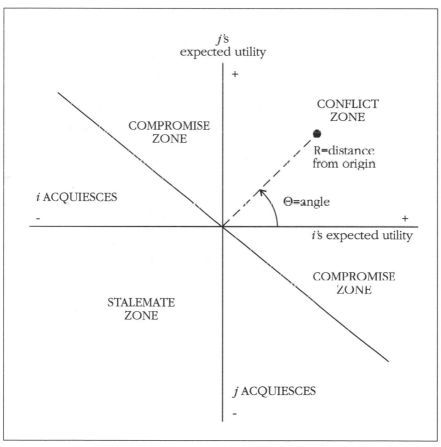

FIGURE B.I
EXPECTATIONS AND PREDICTED RELATIONS
BETWEEN PLAYERS

general likelihood of alternative outcomes in accordance with Banks's monotonicity theorem.

When the expected utility values (as perceived by either or both players) favor a challenge by both i and j, then a confrontation is likely in which neither player is inclined to offer concessions or to bargain. Such conflictual situations involve high political costs and great uncertainty regarding the ultimate outcome. Contrarily, when one player expects to gain more by challenging an opponent's position than by doing nothing and the other player anticipates greater losses than gains in a confrontation, then the costs of resolving the issue are greatly reduced and the prospects of an amicable settlement are enhanced. If one player expects to gain more than the other is prepared to yield, then there is an opportunity to negotiate over the difference in expectations. If one player anticipates losing *more* than the other believes it stands to gain, then we expect that the player anticipating a loss gives in to its opponent's demands. Finally, if each player believes there is more to be lost than gained by challenging the other's position, then the status quo between them is expected to prevail. In this case any demands or proposals made are likely to be mere bluffs and bluster not backed up by credible substance. By examining the distribution of information in graphs like figure B.1, it is possible to estimate how each player will behave and with what consequences.

What information does the perceptual model reveal? Recall that every player (decision maker) is assumed to know the array of positions, potential power, and salience of every other player. That information is common knowledge. The private information possessed by each player involves the shape of its own utility function and the belief it holds about the expected utilities of each other player. Thus, everyone is assumed to know the basic information that goes into the expected utility model.

The beliefs of each player imply actions. Those actions, in extracting or granting concessions over support for this or that specific position, lead each player to reevaluate the situation. As players (stakeholders) respond to revised proposals, their responses are supported by their beliefs and expectations. The prospects for a favorable or unfavorable settlement change for many participants as a consequence of responses to proposals. Beliefs and expectations provide the foundation for a quasi-dynamic assessment of the evolution of issue positions and to recalculations of the location of the median voter.

When players are persuaded or coerced into accepting a proposal different from their initial (or current) position on an issue, the decision process enters a new phase. Coalitions change, and the support or risks associated with alternative proposals vary. New proposals are brought forward as revised beliefs and expectations open new possibilities or foreclose old ones. Each such sequence of revised stances on an issue is called an *iteration* or *bargaining round* (the terms are used interchangeably). The expected utility model computes as many iterations as it takes for the policy issue to reach a stable outcome—an outcome from which there seems to be no meaningful possibility of change given the estimated expectations of the players.

The expected utility model portrays a process of decision making during each iteration. To gain a sense of what happens within the logic of the model during each iteration, think of the players as being engaged in a peculiar game of cards. At the outset, each player is dealt a hand, the quality of which depends on the commonly known characteristics of the player. Stronger players (or those with strong backing from others) generally are dealt better hands than weaker players. Because of variations in salience, some players pay closer attention to their cards than do others and so form different perceptions of the situation. Based on the cards they hold and the known characteristics of other players, each player forms perceptions about how good each opponent's hand is relative to its own. On that basis, each player decides what proposals or bids to make to the other player(s).

If a player believes his or her hand is very weak compared to a specific opponent's, then no proposal is made to that opponent. If i expects to lose to j, for instance, then i does not make a proposal to j. If, however, i thinks it holds a good hand relative to j, then i makes a proposal in the form of a suggested change in position by j on the issue at hand.[4] If i thinks j stands to lose quite a lot, then i will propose that j accept i's current position.[5] If i thinks it has a hand good enough to shift j's position but not so good that j will give in to what i wants, then i proposes a compromise somewhere between i's position and j's.[6]

---

4. Player i makes a proposal if the conjunction of i's expected utility and i's estimate of j's expected utility falls between zero degrees and 45 degrees, or between 270 degrees and 360 degrees, from the horizontal axis. That is the domain within which i believes it has a comparative advantage over j; and i expects more gains than losses from challenging j's position.

5. A proposed acquiescence or capitulation by j to i's wishes is made if i locates the conjunction of the respective expected utilities in the wedge that falls between 270 degrees and 315 degrees below the horizontal axis in the polar coordinate space or in the wedge between zero degrees and 45 degrees. In the latter instance, i expects resistance from j, but i believes it can enforce its demand. In the former case, i expects no resistance from j.

6. A compromise is proposed if i believes the conjunction of the relevant ex-

After all the players have submitted their secret proposals to one another, each player now reviews the new cards—the proposals—that it holds. Of course, some proposals are better for the recipient than others. Indeed, some proposals turn out to be frivolous in that the proposer cannot enforce the proposal, something that the proposer might learn only at the end of the round of proposal making. Other proposals received by a decision maker are potentially enforceable but fall by the wayside because a superior, enforceable proposal was made by a different player. Each player would like to choose the best offer made to it, and each proposer enforces its bids to the extent that it can. Those better able to enforce their wishes than others can make their proposals stick. Given equally enforceable proposals, players move the least that they can. Each player selects from among the bids it made and the bids it received. The bid chosen is the proposal that is the optimal choice for the player given the constraints under which it operates. These constraints include its own perceptions and the reality of which proposals turn out to be enforceable and which turn out to be beaten back by opponents or rejected outright as unenforceable by the recipient.

In a round of proposal making, players learn new information about their opponents. If, for instance, a player finds that some proposals it thought of as enforceable are successfully rejected, then it learns the proposal was unenforceable (i.e., the player has less support than it thought). By monitoring responses to its proposals, a player learns how much leverage it has with other players. If a proposal is accepted, then a player learns that it made the best offer among all the proposals made to the recipient of its accepted bid.

When the players finish sorting out their choices among proposals, each shifts to the position contained in the proposal it accepted. Of course, when a player agrees to a compromise, it hopes that the other player will also live up to its end of the bargain. But in this game promises are not binding. Proposals are enforceable if a player has the wherewithal to compel another player to do what it says it will do. Each player is free to renege on a proposed deal as long as it can enforce some other agreement or as long as someone else can enforce another agreement.

What consequences follow from the actions implied by the first iteration through the model? How do those actions influence the location of the median voter? How do we determine when the median voter outcome at a particular iteration is to be taken as the resolution of the issue

pected utilities falls between 315 degrees and 360 degrees from the horizontal axis in the polar coordinate figure.

at hand? If no player believes it has a remaining credible proposal, then the game ends. Similarly, if the value of remaining proposals is so small that the cost of continuing to bargain outweighs the value for each player of the expected improvement in the outcome, then the game ends, and the policy position of the median voter of that stage of the game is the predicted policy outcome. If, however, credible proposals are believed to remain, then the game continues. (For a fuller description of the sequential process in this game, we suggest seeing Bueno de Mesquita and Stokman, 1994.)

How Can The Model Be Estimated?
A General Approach to Developing the Data

Political outcomes—whether they involve intra- or intergovernmental relations or negotiations between public and private organizations or even within a single organization—can be and have been explained and predicted using the model delineated above. To do so, however, requires converting theoretical concepts into practical application. Although this can be extremely difficult, there is, fortunately, a body of knowledge that can be called on to estimate the critical variables. By combining the perspective of this rational-actor model with the knowledge and expertise of area or issue experts, it is possible to estimate the variables of interest and to solve the perceptual and "voting" components of the model discussed here.

The forecasting and perceptual models require the identification of the players (groups, stakeholders, decision makers, ...) interested in trying to influence a policy outcome on the issues in question. For each player, data must then be estimated on three variables: preferred outcome, capabilities, and salience. Sometimes, in institutionally structured settings, it is also important to take into account structural constraints that operate to help shape outcomes. With just this minimal information in hand, and *without any other information,* regarding, for instance, the history of the situation, the history of relations between particular players within the situation, other sunk costs, and without even interviewing the players involved to assess their judgments about beliefs and expectations, it is possible to predict what the likely actions and outcome will be. This is true whether the issues being investigated are well defined and structured or whether the issues and their institutional setting are less clearly set out.

Where are the necessary data estimates to come from? Probably the best source is individuals with area or issue expertise. Such individuals have great insight into who the players are likely to be on an issue. What is more, although area experts often doubt that they possess the essential information to quantify capabilities or salience, through careful interactive techniques it is generally possible to elicit such information. The essential features behind the development of such estimates is to begin by identifying the most powerful player and assigning that player a capability score of 100. All other players can then be rated in proportion to the most capable player and in proportion to each other. Issues must be defined precisely enough so that players' preferences can be located on a continuum. This also is not particularly problematic for suitably trained investigators.

The full details of such estimation techniques are too lengthy to enumerate here. Nevertheless, it should be noted that it is possible to achieve a very high level of accuracy and cross-expert agreement on the essential information, even when the experts in question disagree markedly with one another on the likely outcome or evolution of discussion on an issue. The greatest power and insight from such an approach can be attained by combining the analytic consistency of models such as those explained here with the nuanced and rich insights of area or issue experts.

When issue experts combine their skills with the analytic strengths of these models, then accurate and subtle predictions are most likely to be attained. To be sure, an abstract model such as the one proposed here is of no value without the information from experts needed to turn its abstractions into practical estimates. Expert knowledge, of course, is quite valuable even without a model to suggest what information is critical and how that information should be organized. But, in numerous controlled experiments it has been found that the predictions extracted from the model in conjunction with the information from area experts is substantially more reliable than the predictions made by the experts themselves. After all, most area specialists have invested heavily in learning critical facts about the place they study. They usually have invested less time in developing expertise in theories of decision making under uncertainty. It is insights from just such theories that this model incorporates and routinizes.

Model Output

The preceding discussion provides an abstract sense of the modeling process incorporated in the expected utility model. Here we discuss the elements of the model's extensive output and what its results tell us about politics. Table B.1 presents an example of the data required by the model. These data were assembled in examining the question, "What is the attitude of each stakeholder with regard to whether the Hong Kong

TABLE B.1

DATA INPUTS

Group	Resources	Position	Salience	Long name
USA	.3	100	.85	United States
ROC	.1	100	.4	Taiwan
Demp	.15	91	.9	Democratic politicians
HKCS	.4	85	.8	Hong Kong Civil Service
IntB	.6	85	.6	International business
BigB	.4	85	.3	Big local business
Sbus	.3	75	.3	Small local business
ProC	.25	75	.3	Pro–People's Republic politicians
PLA	.7	63	.6	People's Liberation Army
Prov	.4	63	.7	Provinces
Prog	1.	50	.9	Chinese progressives
Cons	.4	36	.9	Chinese conservatives

dollar should continue to be pegged to the U.S. dollar?" Each stake-holder's preferred issue position is expressed on a numeric scale. The value 36 on that scale represents the position that the Hong Kong dollar should no longer be pegged to the U.S. dollar. The value 50 represents the position that the currency peg should be maintained only as long as it comes at a low cost. The value 100 represents the position that the Hong Kong dollar should be fully convertible; thus the value 100 represents the status quo.

The initial data yield predictions about relationships (as already suggested). These relationships are expressed both numerically and verbally in the results generated by the model. For instance, the PLA prefers to weaken the conditions under which the Hong Kong dollar would not be pegged to the United States dollar. The status quo is 100, while the PLA desires a weakened peg equal to 63 on the issue continuum scale. The United States favors the status quo. Solving the expected utility model leads to the calculation that the PLA's expected utility for making a proposal to the United States to weaken the peg is equal to −0.384. That is, the PLA believes it should not challenge the United States on this issue. At the same time, the PLA does not fear pressure from the United States. The model indicates that the PLA believes the United States's expected utility for challenging the PLA's position is −0.439. So, according to the logic of the expected utility model, the PLA anticipates that there will be a *stalemate* between the views of the United States and its own views regarding how fully the Hong Kong dollar should be pegged to the American dollar.

The expected utility model also calculates the perceived relationship between the PLA and the United States from the American point of view. The model's logic leads to the calculation that the United States's expected utility for challenging the PLA's position in favor of a weakened peg equals 0.405 from the American perspective. The PLA's expected utility in the same comparison equals 0.394 from the American point of view. That is, the expected utility model's estimates indicate that the United States would try to pressure the PLA to uphold the status quo and that the United States expects a political *conflict* with the PLA over this issue. Additionally, the model calculates what the likely consequence is of the interaction of the PLA's perspective (stalemate) and the American perspective (conflict). The model's output reports that the interaction of these two perspectives will produce a small concession by the PLA. The PLA is predicted to *compromise* by altering its policy stance from its initial position of 63 on the scale. It will support a slightly stronger peg than it truly wants. The model predicts the PLA shifts to 68 on the scale in response to American pressure.

Of course, the model does not only assess the relationship between the United States and the PLA. It evaluates the perceptions and interactions of every pair of players (stakeholders). It predicts the proposals made to each, viewed as credible by each, accepted and rejected by each, and the consequence of policy shifts on the predicted final policy outcome. For example, the model predicts that large local Chinese business interests, who initially favor only a small weakening of the peg (from 100 to 85), will quickly shift their position to support the PLA's initial approach. The large local Chinese business interests shift from 85 on the issue scale to 63. In part because of the PLA's willingness to back a considerably weakened peg, its position in a subsequent bargaining round is predicted to retreat to 63. The PLA reneges on the concessions it is predicted to grant to the United States in the first bargaining round.

The example of the relationship between the United States and the PLA highlights an important feature of the expected utility model. It is noteworthy that the model predicts how the PLA perceives its relationship with the United States (and with all other stakeholders) and how the United States perceives its relationship with the PLA (and with all other stakeholders). By estimating these perceptions, the expected utility model facilitates identifying circumstances in which decision makers overestimate or underestimate their potential to persuade others to change their policy stance on the issues in question. The model's output includes tables that summarize not only the proposals that get made, but also any proposals that would have been credible and could have been made but are not expected to be made because of a perceptual error on the part of a stakeholder. For instance, the Chinese conservatives, who favor eliminating the peg between the Hong Kong dollar and the United States dollar (position 36 on the issue continuum), perceive their relationship with the PLA to be a stalemate. Consequently, they are not expected to seek support for their policy preference from the PLA. The expected utility model indicates that the PLA is prepared to compromise with the conservatives if it is pressured to do so. According to the expected utility model, the PLA could be persuaded by the conservatives to support a policy equivalent to position 55 on the issue scale. Of course, if it is not challenged by the conservatives, the PLA will not volunteer to make this concession. The conservatives fail to recognize that the PLA perceives itself to be vulnerable to them. As a result, the conservatives fail to capitalize on an opportunity to improve the policy outcome from their point of view.

Taking into account the challenges that are recognized, the expected utility model output reports that the status quo at 100 will erode a year or so after Hong Kong reverts to China. The peg to the United States dollar will be weakened from 100 on the scale to 68. A year or so beyond that initial erosion, the peg will be weakened a little more, to 63 on the scale. This means that the Chinese will weaken the Hong Kong dollar's dependence on the value of the United States dollar whenever maintaining the peg proves politically or economically costly to the Chinese government.

It should be evident from this discussion that the expected utility model's output is quite detailed. The model can require several iterations to resolve an issue, although for most issues a stable predicted outcome is arrived at after two or three bargaining rounds. Even with as few as two or three iterations, the printout can include more than a hundred pages of detailed information on the relationship between every pair of stakeholders. The printout includes numerical estimates of expected utilities and verbal interpretations of those numerical estimates. The printout reports each stakeholder's propensity to take risks and the perceived relationship of each player toward each other player. From that perceptual information, the model also reports in the printout what the consequences of the interaction of stakeholders is anticipated to be. The printout reports the proposals made by each stakeholder to each other stakeholder and the credibility of each proposal, and it identifies specific proposals that could have credibly been made but were not recognized by the relevant stakeholder. The printout also reports the shift in each stakeholder's policy position during each iteration and the predicted outcome of the issue during each bargaining round. The printout reports when bargaining is predicted to end and what the final policy choice is expected to be. With so much detail, the expected utility model facilitates not only accurate prediction but also the construction of strategic scenarios that stakeholders can use to alter the anticipated policy outcome by taking advantage of the opportunities to make proposals that, without the expected utility model, they were likely to overlook because of perceptual errors.

Sample of Published Predictions

Listed here, in inverse chronological order, are illustrative predictive studies (papers, articles, books) based on the expected utility model discussed in this book.

ALSARABATI, CAROL, AND MARK ABDOLLAHIAN

    1995 "The Middle East: Israel, the Arabs, and the Prospects for Peace." American Political Science Association meeting, Chicago. September.

ARBETMAN, MARINA

    1995 "Evolving Property Relations: Australian Aborigines and Modernity." American Political Science Association meeting, Chicago. September.

FUCHS, DORIS, JACEK KUGLER, AND HARRY PACHON

    1995 "Mexico: NAFTA, Elections, and the Future of Economic and Poltical Reform." American Political Science Association meeting, Chicago. September.

JAMES, PATRICK, AND MICHAEL LUSZTIG

    1995 "Canada: Predicting Quebec's Economic and Political Future within North America." American Political Science Association meeting, Chicago. September.

ORGANSKI, A.F.K.

    1995 "The Future Settlement of Jerusalem." American Political Science Association meeting, Chicago. September.

BUENO DE MESQUITA, BRUCE, AND FRANS STOKMAN, EDS.

    1994 *European Community Decision Making.* New Haven: Yale University Press. This work compares the model used here to models developed by James Coleman, Frans Stokman, Reinier Van Osten, and Jan Van Den Bos in the context of European Community decisions regarding automobile regulations, air transport harmonization, bank policy, and regulation of radioactive emissions.

FRIEDMAN, FRANCINE

    1994 "To Fight or Not to Fight: The Decision to Settle the Croat-Serb Conflict." Proceedings, Indiana Political Science Association meeting.

BUENO DE MESQUITA, BRUCE, AND SAMUEL S.G. WU

    1994 "Assessing the Dispute in the South China Sea: A Model of

China's Security Decision Making." *International Studies Quarterly,* September, 379–403.

NEWMAN, DAVID, AND BRIAN BRIDGES
1994   "North Korean Nuclear Weapons Policy: An Expected Utility Study." *Pacific Focus,* Fall, 61–80.

BUENO DE MESQUITA, BRUCE, JAMES MORROW, AND SAMUEL S.G. WU
1993   "Forecasting the Risks of Nuclear Proliferation: Taiwan as an Illustration of the Method," *Security Studies* 2 (Spring/ Summer): 311–31.

ORGANSKI, A.F.K., AND BRUCE BUENO DE MESQUITA
1993   "Forecasting the 1992 French Referendum." *In New Diplomacy in the Post–Cold War World,* ed. Roger Morgan, Jochen Lorentzen, and Anna Leander, 67–75. New York: St. Martin's Press.

BUENO DE MESQUITA, BRUCE, AND A.F.K. ORGANSKI
1992   "A Mark in Time Saves *Nein:* An Illustration of a Forecasting Method Using Formal Models." *International Political Science Review,* 81–100.

BUENO DE MESQUITA, BRUCE, AND CHAE-HAN KIM
1991   "Prospects for a New Regional Order in Northeast Asia." *Korean Journal of Defense Analysis,* Winter, 65–82.

BUENO DE MESQUITA, BRUCE
1990   "Multilateral Negotiations: A Spatial Analysis of the Arab-Israeli Dispute." *International Organization,* Summer, 317–40.

FEDER, STANLEY
1987   "Factions and Policon: New Ways to Analyze Politics." *Studies in Intelligence,* Spring, 41–57. This work surveys dozens of U.S. government applications of the expected utility model and evaluates its accuracy.

BECK, DOUGLAS, AND BRUCE BUENO DE MESQUITA
1985   "Forecasting Policy Decisions: An Expected Utility Approach." In *Corporate Crisis Management,* ed. S. Andriole, 103–22. Princeton, N.J.: Petrocelli Books. This work makes predictions regarding Italian governmental stability and budget deficit policy.

BUENO DE MESQUITA, BRUCE
   1984 "Forecasting Policy Decisions: An Expected Utility Approach to
        Post-Khomeini Iran." *PS*, 226–36.

BUENO DE MESQUITA, BRUCE
   1982 "A Conversation with Bruce Bueno de Mesquita: Where War Is
        Likely in the Next Year or Two." *U.S. News and World Report*,
        3 May, 30.

BUENO DE MESQUITA, BRUCE, AND BRUCE D. BERKOWITZ
   1979 "How to Make a Lasting Peace in the Middle East." *Rochester
        Review*, Spring, 12–18.

Index